SIGNS &
WONDERS
in Ministry Today

EDITED BY

Benny C.
AKER

Gary B.
M^CGEE

Foreword by Thomas E. Trask

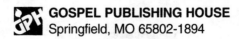

GOSPEL PUBLISHING HOUSE
Springfield, MO 65802-1894

02-0346

©1996 by Gospel Publishing House, Springfield, Missouri 65802-1894. All rights reserved. No part of this book may be reproduced, stored in a retrieval system, or transmitted in any form or by any means—electronic, mechanical, photocopy, recording, or otherwise—without prior written permission of the copyright owner, except brief quotations used in connection with reviews in magazines or newspapers.

Library of Congress Cataloging-in-Publication Data

Signs and wonders in ministry today / edited by Benny C. Aker, Gary B. McGee
     p.   cm.
    Includes bibliographical references.
    ISBN 0-88243-346-6
    1. Pentecostal churches. 2. Pentecostal churches—Missions.
3. Evangelistic work. 4. Holy Spirit. 5. Revivals. 6. Miracles. 7 Gifts.
Spiritual. 8. Spiritual warfare. 9. Spiritual healing. 10. Assemblies of
God.   I. Aker, Benny C., 1939–   II. McGee, Gary B.,
1945–
BX8762.Z5S54   1996
289.9'4—dc20

                                  96-5869
                                  CIP

Printed in the United States of America

Contents

List of Contributors

Benny C. Aker (Ph.D., Saint Louis University), Professor of New Testament and Exegesis

Roger D. Cotton (Th.D., Concordia Seminary), Professor of Old Testament

James D. Hernando (Ph.D., Drew University), Professor of New Testament

Gary A. Kellner (Ph.D. Cand., Emory University), Director of Extension Education and Assistant Professor of Historical Theology

Edgar R. Lee (S.T.D., Emory University), Academic Dean and Professor of Practical Theology

Gary B. McGee (Ph.D., Saint Louis University), Professor of Church History

Del Tarr (Ph.D., University of Minnesota), President and Professor of Cross-Cultural Communications and Anthropology

R. Paul Wood (D.Min., Texas Christian University), Professor of Missions

Wardine Wood (Ed.D. Cand., Nova University), Adjunct Instructor in Missions Education

Foreword

More than ever before, Pentecostal churches need a new visitation of divine power for enablement to reach lost men and women with the life-changing gospel of Jesus Christ at home and around the world. Today, Pentecostal pastors and laypersons too frequently feel the frustration of spiritual powerlessness and long for a mighty moving of God's Spirit in revival power.

The Scriptures record that first-century Christians witnessed the promised "signs" (exorcisms, healings, speaking in tongues, miracles) as they proclaimed the good news (Mark 16:17–18). Indeed, the New Testament pattern of ministry must be the standard for evangelism and church planting today—the kind of ministry that impacts people in body, soul, and spirit. Furthermore, it rests squarely on the foundational truth that "Jesus Christ [is] the same yesterday, and today, and for ever" (Hebrews 13:8, KJV).

Ministry in the power and gifts of the Spirit must be grounded in God's Word. The famed British Pentecostal Donald Gee once cautioned that "the Word without the Spirit will cause you to dry up. The Spirit without the Word will cause you to blow up. The Word and the Spirit will cause you to grow up." The apostle Paul reminded the Corinthian Christians that "my speech and my preaching was not with enticing words of man's wisdom, but in demonstration of the Spirit and of power" (1 Corinthians 2:4, KJV). This dependence on and anointing of the Spirit energize and accomplish the work of the kingdom of God.

Let us earnestly wait upon the Lord to be clothed with His transforming power to be more effective stewards of the good news.

Dedicated to seeking Pentecostal revival and evangelism, faculty members at Assemblies of God Theological Seminary have prepared a series of biblical, historical, and practical essays that encourage believers to seek for signs and wonders in ministry, answer questions that have surfaced about ministry in the power of the Spirit, and provide practical insights for such ministry. For pastors, missionaries, students, and scholars, *Signs and Wonders in Ministry Today* will be an indispensable resource, but more than that, it will be relevant reading for anyone whose heart is burdened to evangelize our world.

—THOMAS E. TRASK
General Superintendent
General Council of the
Assemblies of God

Preface

What does it mean to be Pentecostal or charismatic? While various distinctives could be mentioned, Pentecostals and charismatics expect the preaching of the gospel to be accompanied by miraculous signs and wonders that will point unbelievers to the transforming power of Jesus Christ. Today on the world scene, large sectors of Christians have become Pentecostal in worship and evangelism. But despite great successes in evangelism and missions, questions linger about ministry in the power and demonstration of the Spirit that challenge Pentecostal spirituality and identity. Although many popular books, magazine articles, and tapes are currently available on the subject, faculty members at the Assemblies of God Theological Seminary concluded that a new study of miracles in ministry merited publication, one that examines biblical foundations, offers practical insights, and provides a historical backdrop.

The production of a book is a team effort in which not all of the contributors are immediately detectable to the readers. For this reason, we express sincere thanks to David Womack, Ministry Resources Development manager, for his encouragement in the project. We also keenly appreciate the skills and expertise of the Book Editing staff of Gospel Publishing House, particularly Glen Ellard, Jean Lawson, Stacie Agee, and Kim Kelley, who have greatly enhanced our efforts.

1

The Church and the Spirit's Power

Del Tarr

Years ago, a mighty move of the Holy Spirit in Burkina Faso, West Africa, totally changed my life and convinced me of the power of Pentecost. Missionaries and national pastors had been praying and fasting for weeks for the Spirit's outpouring, because less than a third of the fifteen thousand Christians in the Assemblies of God there had been baptized in the Holy Spirit. Early one morning, Jacques Kabore woke up everyone at the Bible school in Nagabagre. Kabore had been praying that he too might be Spirit baptized and empowered for ministry in signs and wonders before graduation. And at a quarter past two in the morning, he began singing in tongues, and with his leather lungs, he didn't need a microphone. Everyone woke up—missionaries, national pastors, and students—and went to the chapel.

The meetings continued for three months, twenty-four hours a day. At the end of those ninety days, twenty-five hundred people had been baptized in the Spirit and thirty-five hundred won to Christ by these newly Spirit-filled believers. Even Muslims, drawn to the chapel by the loud praying, soon found themselves unable to stand on their feet because of God's mighty power. Fearing for their lives and prostrate on the floor, they asked Christians praying nearby, "What is this?" To which the Christians responded, "It is the power of Jesus." "But we don't believe in Jesus as Savior," the Muslims answered. "Do you believe in Him now?" the Christians would ask. "Yes, we must

9

believe or die in our sins." Within a few minutes of confessing the lordship of Christ, they would begin speaking in tongues, having been baptized in the Holy Spirit as well.

This revival has continued. From fifteen thousand members, the church has grown to over four hundred thousand, and runs on the wheels of a hundred thousand women who fast and pray every Monday. At this rate, a million people—one of every eight in Burkina Faso—will know Jesus Christ by the year 2000. Significantly, the focus has been less on tongues than on holiness, dealing with sin in Christ's body. Many Christians in the initial revival, when submitting themselves to the Spirit, would suddenly get up, borrow a bicycle, and leave for two or three days. After returning, their testimonies had a similar ring: "I remembered during prayer of stealing two chickens at a town thirty kilometers from here. So I went there and finding the victim, said, 'I want God's Holy Spirit. I won't receive His blessing because three years ago I stole two chickens from you. Here are the two chickens.'" After confessing their sins and repenting, they would begin, right there, speaking in tongues. Next, they explained the way of salvation to their hearers and "the amazing thing is they would get saved and in a few minutes speak in tongues as well."

Preparation for Spiritual Warfare

Aspects of the revival convinced me that some of Satan's territories cannot be penetrated without the power of the Holy Spirit in signs and wonders. Most ministers outside of Pentecostal and charismatic ranks have not been prepared for Spirit-empowered ministry.[1] Kirk Bottomly, a Presbyterian pastor, lamented, "We are generally trained to know about God, but not to know God or to do the work of God."[2] Roger Barrier, a Baptist minister, recalled that neither his upbringing in church nor his seminary training ever prepared him to pray for the sick as instructed in James 5:13–16.[3]

Unfortunately, hesitations about ministry in the power of the Spirit can also be found in Pentecostal ranks. Third- and fourth-generation Pentecostals ask the same question that troubled Elisha after his master had been taken in a fiery chariot to heaven: "Where now is the Lord, the God of Elijah?" Having heard about the miracles in the early Pentecostal movement and the accounts of power-filled revivals in years gone by, and having read about signs and wonders happening on missions fields, their hearts cry out, "Lord, do it again!" "Let me see it in my ministry!" "Let my congregation experience Pentecost so our community can be won to Christ!"

While we honor the many contributions of evangelical theologians, wrestling with principalities and powers of the air (Ephesians 6:12) demands that God's servants have more than exegetical skills and doctrinal training; they must be spiritually equipped for spiritual warfare. Experiencing the reality of Pentecost, however, does more than fill spiritual reservoirs; it empowers believers to bless others with the good news of the gospel and to confront demonic forces that bind people in their sins. Before Jesus ascended, He promised His disciples, "You will receive power when the Holy Spirit comes on you; and you will be my witnesses in Jerusalem, and in all Judea and Samaria, and to the ends of the earth" (Acts 1:8).

At the beginning of the twentieth century, Pentecostalism came on the crest of a worldwide revival. While several holiness denominations became Pentecostal (the Church of God in Christ, the Church of God [Cleveland, Tennessee], and the Pentecostal Holiness Church), new organizations and networks soon formed: the Assemblies of God, the International Church of the Four-square Gospel, the Pentecostal Assemblies of Canada, and the Pentecostal Free Will Baptist Church, among many others. All committed themselves to world evangelization in the power of the Spirit in the last days. Now many decades older, Pentecostals face the threat of third- and fourth-generational decline in spiritual zeal. Some observers suspect that denominational Pentecostals have begun moving into a post-Pentecostal phase of their existence.

Why should this be? Why do fervent witness and expectant faith for miracles diminish? Why have American Pentecostals become satisfied with just maintaining creedal loyalty to the full gospel distinctive, especially when so many sister churches overseas have kept the same doctrinal fidelity and continue in revival and growth?

Pentecostals Need Revival

Several experts provide insights into why contemporary Pentecostals need revival if they hope to maintain their traditional spiritual vitality and quicken the pace of their evangelism and growth. Sociologist Margaret Poloma believes that denominational successes lessen Pentecostals' healthy fear of institutionalization. Organizations by nature accommodate themselves to the prevailing culture (e.g., management models, flow charts, salary scales, technology) and, in this case, move the churches away from the charismatic leadership and the spiritual energy that brought them into being and animated them for so long.[4] Church-growth authority C. Peter Wagner suggests that Pentecostal distinctives have been negatively affected through the mainstreaming of Pentecostal denominations into the National Association of Evangelicals. He detects that over the years there has been "a gradual de-emphasizing of the signs, wonders and other miraculous ministries so outwardly characteristic of first and early second-generation Pentecostals. Evangelicals could live with the Pentecostals as long as they were polite enough not to raise issues such as speaking in tongues or power ministries in mixed company."[5]

Until recently, many evangelical theologians have taken the cessationist perspective that miracles and the charismata ended before A.D. 100. In Pentecostal schools, evangelical textbooks on exegesis, doctrine, worship, discipleship, and missiology have resulted in the "evangelicalization" of the Movement over the past fifty years. In part, this has resulted in theologically trained, Pentecostal candidates for the ministry who have serious uncertainties about the Spirit's manifestations. Theologian Jon Ruthven's recent critique of cessationism,[6] as well as Paul A. Pomerville's contention that it has impaired the Spirit's ministry in evangelical missiology, has clearly raised a warning signal to Pentecostals: While firmly evangelical in doctrine, they must retain Pentecostal emphases on the baptism in the Holy Spirit with speaking in tongues, the charismata, and signs and wonders in the life and mission of the Church. Indeed, these spiritual dynamics serve as a corrective to evangelical misgivings about ministry in the power of the Spirit.[7]

Many current Pentecostals grew up in the church; they are

children or grandchildren of adults who made hard choices in joining a rather persecuted band of believers. To the latter, the miraculous power of the New Testament Church was normative if a church wanted to see growth. Because of this, they were usually asked to leave their churches. Their children, however, have not faced such tough choices, nor have they experienced the intense alienation from their evangelical brothers and sisters that earlier Pentecostals did. Instead, third- and fourth-generation Pentecostals have readily accepted enculturation into American society, seeking comfortable lifestyles, recognition, power, and financial security. Unwittingly, this has often numbed them to the cost of true discipleship. History shows that all churches and revival movements have struggled with cultural accommodation and their original spiritual vision dimming in succeeding generations.

March 1995

Recognizing the spiritual conflict troubling pastors and congregations, Assemblies of God Theological Seminary has committed itself to leading the way to Pentecostal renewal by training Spirit-filled leaders: the Seminary scripturally addresses burning issues and provides forums for the discussion of controversial issues and errors that follow any revival movement. This prompted the Seminary community to sponsor the "Signs and Wonders" conference in Springfield, Missouri, during March 4–7, 1995. A rich diversity of Assemblies of God and charismatic leaders addressed the topic. The Spirit of God moved mightily, with church officials, pastors, faculty members, and students experiencing a signal visitation of God's power as they worshiped and prayed. Healing testimonies quickly surfaced: A woman who had suffered for twenty years with a whiplash injury from an accident testified on the first night that "after Pat Robertson finished preaching, he said that God was healing someone who had been injured with a whiplash injury. Immediately, all the pain left my neck and shoulder!"

The healing of reconciliation also took place. A Nebraska minister described an unplanned encounter with a couple who had preceded him in his pastorate: "They had left under a tremendous load of pain caused by some who attended the church at that time. The spirit of forgiveness in the meeting led him to seek a time of fellowship with me. As the current pastor, I had the privilege and blessing of the Lord to formally apologize on behalf of my congregation." Through tears of joy, a chapter of hurt and pain in the life of this couple and their former congregation was closed.

After returning home, pastors reported remarkable revival services in their churches, sometimes lasting three and four hours. Scores of people were saved, delivered, baptized, or renewed in the Spirit, and dozens were healed. One pastor said, "Surely, God has launched our Movement into a new and fresh dimension of 'Spirit and Word' leadership. We have seen nearly twenty people baptized in the Holy Spirit, and nearly fifty accepted Christ during the past two weeks."

Thousands of Pentecostal churches in North America desperately need a powerful move of the Holy Spirit. Critical reflection can no longer be avoided. Just as the Scriptures teach Christians to be self-critical before receiving Communion, Spirit-filled believers must ask hard questions: What might God be saying to my church, to my denomination or network of churches? How can evil powers be confronted in our culture? What can we do to reverse the decline in Pentecostal church growth in America? How can spiritual unity break through to bring about God's victory in our communities and nation? Self-examination leads to spiritual health.

Early Pentecostals committed themselves to following New Testament methods in evangelism.[8] Does that commitment still live in our hearts? Ministry in the power of the Spirit has never been more needed for effective evangelism and church planting than it is today. Effective Pentecostal evangelism, however, necessitates unity in the Spirit—harmony among believers. As Jesus said to His disciples, "A new command I give you: Love one another. As I have loved you, so you must love one another. By this all men will know that you are my disciples, if you love one another" (John 13:34–35).

Diversity versus Unity

Pentecostals have not been generous to diversity. Question: Did any good come from the Latter Rain movement in the late

1940s, which brought new—and controversial—interest in the gifts of the Spirit?[9] Was God trying to speak through the movement to other Pentecostals? Yes, to some extent, but most of our churches threw everything out. Did anything good come from the Jesus movement among young people in the 1960s and 1970s?[10] Yes, and the churches that welcomed them with their long hair and ragged clothes found themselves blessed by their fresh spiritual zeal. Did anything good emerge from the charismatic renewal?[11] When the Spirit was poured out on Presbyterians, Episcopalians, and even Roman Catholics, some accused God of having poor aim. More Pentecostal churches accepted it, but thousands rejected it out of hand, and tragically, many still do. "Nothing there," they said, looking only at problem areas. Jack Hayford calls this "small-souledness," referring to the "pride in our own restricted circle and a preoccupation with our own small world that can prey on our spiritual health."[12]

Many Pentecostals have become satisfied with retelling stories of yesterday's revivals and spiritual victories; they are blind to the new outpourings of the Spirit. When this happens, the old wineskins can no longer contain the new wine of the Spirit. Will the current "Toronto Blessing" bear fruit? I'm not ready to tell you that the laughing and roaring characterizing the services at the Airport Vineyard church in Toronto, Canada, should become fixtures in church worship. But recently at a meeting of the Fellowship of Evangelical Seminary Presidents, two Canadians asked me, "What stand are you taking on the Toronto Blessing?" "I don't find biblical examples for some of the phenomena," I responded, and then asked them, "Do you see any fruit from it?" They both replied, "Definitely!" People visiting the Vineyard from their churches—pastors and layleaders—have been transformed. Going back to their churches, some now tithe for the first time, others have traveled overseas as foreign missionaries, and young people have received calls to the ministry. "It's revolutionizing the churches around our seminaries." I added, "Well that's the kind of fruit that should come out of every genuine revival."

In the prologue to the Paris edition of Miles Coverdale's 1538 version of the Scriptures in both Latin and English, Coverdale described the value of comparative Bible translations: "Let this translation be no prejudice to the other. . . . See that one translation declareth, openeth, and illustrateth another. And that in many cases one is a plain commentary to another." More than four and a half centuries later, Christians still squabble over translations. The spirit of exclusiveness hinders revival. Prejudices shatter the unity that worship and fellowship require and also cripple the potential for evangelism with signs and wonders.

Responding to Undesirables

Elitism obscures the very nature of the gospel and restrains the work of the Spirit (Ephesians 2:11–22). When Peter visited the home of Simon the tanner in Joppa, he went up to the roof to pray, where he "fell into a trance." Luke records that "he saw heaven opened and something like a large sheet being let down to earth by its four corners. It contained all kinds of four-footed animals, as well as reptiles of the earth and birds of the air. Then a voice told him, 'Get up, Peter. Kill and eat.' 'Surely not, Lord!' Peter replied. 'I've never eaten anything impure or unclean.' The voice spoke to him a second time, 'Do not call anything impure that God has made clean.' This happened three times and immediately the sheet was taken back to heaven" (Acts 10:11–16). Peter obeyed, and when he preached to Cornelius and his household, "the Holy Spirit came on all who heard the message" (Acts 10:44).

What do you think happened when the Jerusalem church leaders heard the news? It is doubtful that they said to each other, "Thank God. We never thought those Gentile dogs could ever get saved." Rather, one might imagine the actual conversation to have gone something like this: "It has never been done like this." "Peter, you actually went into the house of an uncircumcised man?" "You even ate with them?" In the end, however, the leaders recognized that the Lord had revealed His will, and they endorsed the Gentile mission (Acts 10:1 through 11:18).

Today, many Pentecostals look at that sheet and like Peter reply, "Not so, Lord!" The fallen human nature still runs to exclusion, not inclusion. It builds fences around local congregations (and denominations) to keep out the undesirables—those who don't fit in for whatever reason. Charles Hackett, national director of Home Missions for the Assemblies of God, said in a seminary chapel service, "When revival comes, . . . God will send people you don't like. He won't do it like you are expecting. People who come won't be perfect. Some of your 'Christians' will leave the church."[13]

Unless Pentecostals confront their own spiritual ethnocentricity, they will become stodgy and immovable. The potential of the Spirit's ministry for the life and witness of the Church will always be hampered by saints who spend more energy building walls than tearing them down. Despite Coverdale's insight, many have concluded that approximately a hundred years ago Pentecostals received the "Authorized Version" of all that could ever be known about Pentecost. Only moves of the Spirit that conform to their "edition" receive approval.

Jesus promised that the Spirit would teach believers "all things" (John 14:26), yet when Pentecostals boast about their unequaled insights into the ministry of the Spirit and brag of having a larger share of His power and blessing, pride short-circuits their spiritual power. Paul forthrightly warned the Corinthians that even if they spoke in tongues, gave prophetic utterances, plumbed the deepest mysteries, or by faith moved mountains, without humility and love as the primary motivation, their achievements would merely amount to noisy, clanging sounds and not harmonize with the melody that should sound from God's people (1 Corinthians 13:1–3).

Pentecostal evangelism has achieved spectacular results in many parts of the world over the last several decades, but Pentecostals now boast of their triumphs and have become comfortable under the pile of their traditions. To rediscover the power of the Spirit and witness divine signs and wonders when preaching the gospel, they must humble themselves. Theologian J. I. Packer, a keen observer of the contemporary church scene, states, "All Christians are at once beneficiaries and victims of tradition: beneficiaries who receive nurturing in truth and wisdom from God's faithfulness in past generations, victims who now take for granted things that are needing reexamination because some things were not divine absolutes."[14] Church life recurrently conforms more to the prevailing culture than to scriptural ideals. Yet in spite of their weaknesses and exclusivity, God honors the cries of believers when they repent and seek to be better stewards of His grace. Every generation must rekindle the purifying flames of holiness and Pentecostal power to build up the body of Christ and to extend His kingdom.

Listening to Each Other

When believers humble themselves and repent of their sinful pride, the Spirit prompts them to conform their behaviors to God's Word, to confess their sins to one another, and to learn by dialoguing. This leads to power-packed Christian living and dynamic evangelism. Ironically, some Pentecostals and charismatics fear the word "dialogue," doubting that private or public discussion of controversial matters can ever be productive. Jesus, however, did not retreat from two-way communication and chose to dialogue at length with scribes, Pharisees, Nicodemus, the Samaritan woman, Herod Antipas, and even Pilate. He constantly addressed questions that challenged the thinking and consciences of His hearers. The apostle Paul did the same on Mars' Hill, as well as in synagogues, churches, marketplaces, and even in the courts and prisons in Philippi, Caesarea, and Rome.

Missiologist David J. Hesselgrave writes that engaging in "biblical dialogue" neither compromises revealed truth nor subtracts from it since the attention falls on clear communication of the whole counsel of God.[15] Paul instructed the Colossian believers, "Let the peace of Christ rule [umpire] in your hearts, since as members of one body you were called to peace" (Colossians 3:15). This priority on the welfare of the body of Christ and the openness that it requires takes Christians beneath the veneer of polite conversation to deeply troubling matters that potentially threaten spiritual unity. When problems find resolution, the moving of the Spirit then takes on fresh vibrancy in corporate worship and witness.

When it comes to ministry in the power of the Spirit, Pentecostals, charismatics, and evangelicals tend to voice their various opinions without bothering to listen to each other. In particular, they need to converse about the charismatic gifts and signs and wonders, and grow beyond their uncertainties and fears of emotional excesses. The late David J. DuPlessis, a preeminent leader in the charismatic movement, often remarked, "I'd rather tone down a fanatic than to try to raise the dead!" He once used a fireplace as a vivid illustration of the proper management of the gifts of the Spirit. If there's a fire in the fireplace, hot coals may pop out onto the rug. On one side of the fireplace hang tongs. On the other side is a fire extinguisher. Rather than dousing the entire fire with the extinguisher, a person should use the tongs to pick up the coals and drop them back into the fire. Nevertheless, a lot of people use the extinguisher, ending up with only cold, wet ashes.

River of Blessing

The power of the Holy Spirit has enabled Pentecostals and charismatics to break down Satan's strongholds through gospel preaching with miraculous signs and wonders, resulting in millions around the world confessing Jesus as Lord and Savior. Just as Pentecostals in Burkina Faso have seen a nation-changing revival, so North American Pentecostals, in fact all believers, should continually seek the outpouring of the Holy Spirit.

If the channel of Pentecostal tradition continues to narrow and limit the Spirit's ministry, God's rivers of blessing will flood elsewhere. With simplicity of faith, Jacques Kabore chose to open his heart to the breadth of the Spirit's fullness. Let us choose likewise!

Endnotes

[1]For the classic cessationist argument, see Benjamin B. Warfield, *Counterfeit Miracles* (Edinburgh: Banner of Truth Trust, 1918; reprint 1983).

[2]Kirk Bottomly, "Coming Out of the Hanger: Confessions of an Evangelical Deist," in *The Kingdom and the Power: Are Healing and the Spiritual Gifts Used by Jesus and the Early Church Meant for the Church Today?*, ed. Gary S. Greig and Kevin N. Springer (Ventura, Calif.: Regal Books, 1993), 259.

[3]Roger Barrier, "A Pastor's View of Praying for the Sick and Overcoming the Evil One in the Power of the Spirit," in *Kingdom and the Power,* 219–220.

[4]Margaret M. Poloma, *The Assemblies of God at the Crossroads: Charisma and Institutional Dilemmas* (Knoxville: University of Tennessee Press, 1989).

[5]C. Peter Wagner, "Forward," *Kingdom and the Power,* 15.

[6]Jon Ruthven, *On the Cessation of the Charismata: The Protestant Polemic on Postbiblical Miracles* (Sheffield, U.K.: Sheffield Academic Press, 1993).

[7]Paul A. Pomerville, *The Third Force in Missions* (Peabody, Mass.: Hendrickson Publishers, 1985), 79.

[8]E.g., General Council [Assemblies of God] Minutes, (Combined Minutes), 1914–1917, 9–10; Aimee Semple McPherson, *This Is That* (Los Angeles: Echo Park Evangelistic Association, 1923), 593–594; A. J. Tomlinson, *The Last Great Conflict* (Cleveland, Tenn.: Walter E. Rodgers, 1913), 100–115.

[9]William W. Menzies, *Anointed to Serve: The Story of the Assemblies of God* (Springfield, Mo.: Gospel Publishing House, 1971), 321–325; cf., Richard M. Riss, "The Latter Rain Movement of 1948," *Pneuma: The Journal of the Society for Pentecostal Studies* 4 (Spring 1982): 32–45.

[10]Charles Edwin Jones, "Jesus People," in *Dictionary of Pentecostal and Charismatic Movements,* ed. Stanley M. Burgess, Gary B. McGee, Patrick H. Alexander (Grand Rapids: Zondervan Publishing House, 1988), 491–493.

[11]See Richard Quebedeaux, *The New Charismatics II* (San Francisco: Harper & Row, Publishers, 1983).

[12]Jack W. Hayford, "Seven Signs of Imminent Grace," *Charisma and Christian Life,* December 1995, 66.

[13]Charles Hackett, chapel sermon at the Assemblies of God Theological Seminary, December 1, 1994.

[14]J. I. Packer, "The Comfort of Conservatism," in *Power Religion: The Selling Out of the Evangelical Church?,* ed. Michael Scott Morton (Chicago: Moody Press, 1992), 286–7.

[15]David J. Hesselgrave, *Communicating Christ Cross Culturally,* 2d ed. (Grand Rapids: Zondervan Publishing House, 1991), 139.

2

"Wonderful"—God's Name

Roger D. Cotton

What does the Old Testament teach about signs and wonders? Some people say that the Israelites considered everything a miracle because they didn't have a scientific worldview. It does seem that they attributed much more to God's direct involvement and to other spiritual powers than we do, though our doctrine of divine providence differs little. Despite their willingness to credit God more freely, they reserved the terms "signs" and "wonders" for extraordinary occurrences with a divine message, for they did distinguish between the usual and the unusual, the normal and the spectacular intervention of God for a special purpose.

Most of the themes of the theology of signs and wonders in the Old Testament can be seen in Psalm 145. There, David repeatedly praises God for His great, awesome, miraculous works as the ultimate King and the Creator of the universe. The ideal King is one of the most consistently used images of God in the Old Testament, portraying Him relationally instead of defining Him in systematic, propositional statements. Such an image gives a far richer understanding of God and His relationship with people. It especially affords the proper perspective on God's sovereign power. Nothing can compare with Him. As the eternal yet personal Creator, He purposefully involves himself in His creation, saving and sustaining His creatures. He has delivered His people from bondage and death and will destroy the wicked (vv. 4–14,18–20). God continues to provide for His people and fulfills their expectations as the ultimate benevolent, fatherly Monarch who offers the perfect life of prosperity and security to all in His realm, caring for everyone, from the lowliest to the greatest (vv. 7,9,15–16). Psalm 145 affirms the Lord's goodness, grace, compassion, and love as well as His power. His loving, miraculous acts on behalf of His creation bring Him glory and, ultimately, all creatures will forever praise His holy name (vv. 4,21).

Definitions and Key Terms

The Old Testament teaches that God does signs and wonders to establish that He is the loving Sovereign of the universe who intervenes in the world for the eternal good of His creatures. These phenomena both express and confirm the message of His plan of salvation. Signs and wonders is a category of divine intervention, or miracles, that involves awesome phenomena with a message. The terms for signs and wonders used in the Old Testament refer to supernatural, spectacular acts and events clearly beyond human ability, eliciting awe or amazement in people and pointing to something about God and His saving purpose.[1] The Hebrew words for "greatness," "might," "power," and "awesomeness," when used in reference to God and His works, refer to miracles.

However, three major Hebrew words were used for signs and wonders. *'Oth,* or "sign," refers to something that points beyond itself. In the Bible these events grab people's attention and point to God's presence and promises of grace and power (Exodus 4:8–9).[2] God designates the significance of a sign and often only faith receives it. He may even designate people as signs through some aspect of their lives in relation to His purposes (e.g., Isaiah 8:18; Ezekiel 14:8; 24:24; and Zechariah 3:8). Signs in the Old Testament usually confirmed God's Word and saving purpose. In Deuteronomy 7:19, Moses says that because the Israelites had seen the signs in Egypt, they could be assured that the Lord would continue His purpose in their lives by accomplishing the same victory over the peoples in the Promised Land.

Another noun, *pele',* comes from the more frequently used verb *pala',* which means to do something extraordinary, something not explainable by natural or human activity—a wonder or miracle—usually caused by the supernatural power of God.[3] The verb occurs in Genesis 18:14 in the question, "Is any thing too hard for the Lord?" or "Is any thing too amazingly difficult, too marvelous or supernatural, for God to do—is any thing beyond His ability?" Isaiah calls the promised Savior-King "Wonderful," meaning, "Miraculous, Supernatural, and One whom people marvel at" (9:6). As His name, this identifies His nature as miraculous. He does things that go beyond human ability. In that verse the Savior-King is also called "the Mighty [Warrior] God," identifying Him as a divine, supernatural Deliverer.[4]

The third word, *mophet,* the usual noun for "wonder," used with the word for "sign," seems to combine both this idea of miracle and that of sign. It seems to emphasize that the supernatural event, or wonder, has meaning and significance.

The Creator Who Is Personal

Genesis contains the foundational revelation for the subject of signs and wonders. Genesis 1 teaches much about God through its verbs. The first one, *bara',* to "create," is used in the Old Testament only of God's unprecedented actions. All the universe comes from a supernatural act of God. Often this fact provides the basis for trusting God to fulfill His promise of miraculously intervening to save. For example, because of His "fixed laws of heaven and earth," Israel is assured that He will fulfill His promises to them (Jeremiah 33:25–26). Later in Genesis, God's Spirit hovers over the world, and God speaks the specific formation of the creation in the six creation days. Furthermore, He sees what He has made, proclaims it good, blesses His creatures, and commands them to multiply. God teaches in Genesis 1:26–29 and in chapter 2 that He personally formed and gave life to the first people, creating them in His image and delegating to them authority over the rest of the creatures. This indicates that God made people for intimate, personal fellowship with himself, in which they would exercise privilege, responsibility, and accountability, attributes reserved for humanity alone.

Genesis teaches that God is actively involved in the world, personally ruling over His creation as the ultimate, benevolent, paternal Monarch, caring for and enabling it to fulfill His purposes. God wants to be involved in people's lives in a personal relationship; therefore, His interventions—the supernatural—should be a normal part of human existence, comparable to the involvement of a parent in the life of a child. However, like the interventions of a wise parent, God's help will be carefully timed. He will avoid teaching His child to be irresponsible.

According to scriptural precedent, God's direct, spectacular acts for His people will be carefully chosen and infrequent. More often, God interacts with His creation in unspectacular ways, which should be considered a normal part of life. Natural means can be designated by God as signs to remind us of a divine message according to passages like Genesis 1:14, where God says He created the lights in the sky for signs to mark time into seasons, days, and years; He designated the rainbow as a sign of His covenant with His creatures after the flood, promising nothing like it again (Genesis 9:8–17). His cutting off the Jordan River so the Israelites could cross may have been through natural means, such as a landslide, but the perfect timing of it showed that the Lord was the cause (Joshua 3:15–16). The divine interpretation is accepted only by faith in many situations.

However, the word for "signs" in combination with the word for "wonders" refers to the interventions of God in clearly visible, extraordinary ways—not explainable by natural causes, generating amazement and awe toward the Lord—and tend to carry or confirm a message of His saving purpose. God at times chooses to intervene for His people in ways that display His mighty power and thereby confirm the message about His true nature and purpose. For example, a king could send word to his prison guards to release a certain prisoner, or he could go down to the cell and personally open the door, call the prisoner out, and hand him new clothes and money. The latter more dramatically and clearly connects the king with the release of the prisoner. The direct, physical involvement openly testifies to the king's power and mercy. But either way, the prisoner's release results from the decision of the king.

Genesis 3 then explains humankind's loss of fellowship with God and the promise of its restoration. The harmony of Eden ended because of the sin of putting selfish desires before God's will. But the Lord made it possible for those who humbly seek His involvement in their lives to have it restored. He provided salvation in personal fellowship with himself, which is His ultimate purpose for humanity (3:15). But to those who will not repent and turn to Him, He brings judgment. He personally dealt with Cain by warning him, judging him, and then reassuring him with some kind of supernatural sign, or mark, divinely designating him for protection (Genesis 4:15).

The God Who Confirms His Word and His Messengers

The Lord uses signs and wonders throughout the Old Testament to confirm that He is the only true God of supreme authority and to legitimize the claims of His prophets who speak for Him. He confirmed Abraham as His prophet in Genesis 20:7,17–18 through a healing of Abimelech's household in answer to Abraham's prayer.[5] God gave Moses two miraculous signs (Exodus 4:8; also called "wonders" in verse 21) to perform to convince both the Israelites and the Egyptians that he had been sent by God and that his message was to be believed. The account shows that the Egyptians, like many other ancient Near Eastern peoples, believed in the supernatural and that miracles or spectacular events testified to the power of the gods and the ability of human mediators to manipulate that power through magic.

In the Israelite context, Moses did not manipulate but simply obeyed God and announced His decisions. God does awe-inspiring works for authentication, confirmation, or vindication of His message and His messengers and leaders. The Egyptian magicians soon acknowledged the plagues as "the finger of God" (8:19).[6] The Lord calls the sending of flies on the Egyptians and not on His people a miraculous sign of His presence among them and points out the difference His presence makes (Exodus 8:22–23). Thus He declared His identity as the all-powerful God of all the universe and confirmed His word of salvation.

The manipulative power of magic proved limited when compared to the power of the interventions of the Ruler of Israel, the Holy God; the Egyptian gods appeared powerless before Him.[7] The plagues strengthened the faith of the Israelites and motivated Pharaoh and the Egyptians to obey the Lord's word and let His people go. Nehemiah says the signs and wonders in Egypt made a name for the Lord (Nehemiah 9:10). Furthermore, the Lord promised in Exodus 34:10 to do wonders or miracles that had never been done before—literally, "had not been created yet"—in bringing His people Israel into the Promised Land, so that all the people around would see the testimony of God's saving work.

With the sign of prophecy, God confirmed His Spirit's empowerment of the seventy elders to help Moses (Numbers 11:25). Moses himself had the testimony of the ultimate prophet because of the awesome signs and wonders he performed for the Lord (Deuteronomy 34:10–12). God gave supernatural confirmation of His word to Gideon by sending fire to burn up the sacrifice and by making a fleece wet and then dry (Judges 6:17–23,36–40). He also established the authority of His word for Samson's parents through the angel of the Lord, who "did wondrously," or "performed miraculously," as he ascended in the flame (Judges 13:19–20, KJV).

Perhaps the most famous, miraculous attestation of the Lord's authority as the only One who should be worshiped occurred when He sent fire down on Mount Carmel (1 Kings 18:24,37–39), which also confirmed Elijah as His prophet (cf. 2 Kings 1:10). The miracle on Mount Carmel followed the pronouncement of the drought as God's judgment on Israel's idolatry during King Ahab's reign; the drought began and ended with the word of the Lord through His prophet. This public exposure of the powerlessness of the Canaanite god of the storm or rain and fertility (Baal) proclaimed that the Lord—the true God—controls all creation, including human affairs. Such signs challenged Israel to return to their covenant with the Lord and to listen to His messengers, the prophets.

Another testimony to the Lord's superiority resulted from His providing, through Elisha, supernatural knowledge about situations and guidance, advising the king for the protection of Israel against enemy attack (2 Kings 6:8–12). This spoke to both Israel and other nations of the great inferiority of their own abilities and resources compared to the Lord's.

Two of the most awesome miracles of Elijah and Elisha occurred after the end of their ministries: Elijah's ascent to heaven in a whirlwind and the raising of a dead man after contact with Elisha's bones. (It should be noted in the latter case that despite the many awesome miracles performed through Elisha, God still chose to take him to heaven through a sickness [2 Kings 13:14].)

In another sign in the historical books, God made a shadow go backward as assurance to Hezekiah of the answer to his prayer for healing (2 Kings 20:1–11). Most of the miracles done in the life of a prophet had the effect of authenticating his ministry and message about the Lord and encouraging his faith and the faith of others.

The prophets describe signs that God does in the salvation of His people, which testify to the world of His grace and the judgment of all who do not know Him. Joel promises cosmic signs in the last days, at the culmination of God's salvation and judgment (Joel 2:30–31). Jesus, responding to the Pharisees' insincere demands for a sign, refers to the sign of Jonah (Matthew 12:39–41). He said that the resurrection-like deliverance of Jonah from the fish would find its ultimate expression in Jesus' resurrection, confirming His preaching and the condemnation of those who rejected it.

The Lord's speaking quietly to Elijah at Horeb after sending a rock-shattering wind, an earthquake, and fire implied that he should not serve God simply because of powerful and frightening phenomena. Elijah had to look and listen for Him—His personal presence and voice, His greater good and loving purposes— behind all His miraculous interventions and spectacular phenomena. As signs they point to the Lord; His miracles should inspire humility, faith, and obedience toward Him. Obviously, God's ways differ from ours.

Sometimes God's miracles and signs and wonders functioned as tests for His people (Exodus 15:25–26; Deuteronomy 8:2–5). In Deuteronomy 13:1–5 Moses says: "If a prophet, or one who foretells by dreams, appears among you and announces to you a miraculous sign or wonder, and if the sign or wonder . . . takes place, and he says, 'Let us follow other gods' . . . you must not listen to the words of that prophet or dreamer. The Lord your God is testing you to find out whether you love him with all your heart and with all your soul. . . . That prophet or dreamer must be put to death, because he preached rebellion against the Lord your God, who brought you out of Egypt and redeemed you." This passage suggests that ancient prophets could be expected to perform signs and wonders but denounces them as false if their message leads people away from the Lord.[8] God may use such happenings to determine whether people care as much about their relationship with Him as they do about signs and wonders.

God's people should determine the legitimacy of prophets by whether their words are in accord with the revelation already received about the true nature of God and what He expects of His people. The salvation event of the Exodus laid the foundation for the Israelites' relationship with God and, therefore, always had to be held in focus to keep them from turning away from the true way of eternal life. Regardless of miraculous signs, any prophet whose message led people away from the Lord, who revealed himself in the Exodus and in the covenant given at Sinai, was to be put to death.

The Warrior God Who Saves

Using words that would describe an ancient warrior who conquers his enemy by superior power and skill, Exodus describes God's supernatural intervention to save Israel as He delivered them out of Egypt. In the Exodus, the awesome, divine deliverance of Israel from Egypt through the Red Sea established Israel's faith in the Lord and His servant Moses (Exodus 14:31). The song in Exodus 15 celebrates this, and verse 11 says that such awesome miracle-working power shows that none can be compared to the Lord, the Holy God and Mighty Warrior. Over and over again, the Old Testament Scriptures retell the salvation event, the greatest moment in Israel's history, that made them God's people and demonstrated Him as the only true God. In His supernatural acts of power, He conquered the enemies of His people and showed himself to be the ultimate Deliverer. Most Old Testament references to God's signs and wonders have to do with the Exodus. This great, miraculous intervention of the past then becomes a paradigm of God's salvation plan and a guarantee of the future fulfillment of His promise. In fact, all of God's interventions should reassure believers of His continuing faithfulness to His saving purpose and His power to overcome all opposition.

Throughout the history of Israel, God affirmed His salvation purpose by fighting for them when they sought His help through repentance and faith. Sometimes He empowered them, or sometimes He weakened their enemies. Other times He directly struck the enemy dead or used natural means, including other armies, to rout them. One of the most awesome miracles of nature occurred when the Lord answered Joshua's prayer by doing something to the sunlight, referred to as the sun "standing still," so that they could win in battle (Joshua 10:13). Verse 14 says, "There has never been a day like it before or since, a day when the Lord listened to a man. Surely, the Lord was fighting for Israel!" He is the supreme, divine Warrior who delivers those who have a faith relationship with Him. No enemy can stand before Him. He deals decisively with the powers of evil, sin, and death. He conquers them and brings eternal life to all who accept His offer.

The King Who Leads and Provides

Moses goes on to proclaim in Exodus 15 that God not only saves His people miraculously as the divine Warrior, but leads them to the place of His presence and He reigns as benevolent King forever (v. 18). At Mount Sinai, God established His covenant with Israel as His vassal nation and, as the ideal King, promised to provide wise and just leadership, prosperity, and protection for His people, so they could live in peace and security and enjoy His goodness forever.[9] God provided food and water miraculously in the wilderness and preserved their clothes (Exodus 16 and 17; Deuteronomy 8:4). Moses connects these phenomena with the miraculous signs in Egypt as God's means of teaching His people who He is (Deuteronomy 29:3–6).

Elijah and Elisha performed several miracles that sustained life for Gentiles, including raising the dead, demonstrating that God cares about human need—of all humans—and has the power to meet the ultimate need: deliverance from death. At that time He found hearts more receptive outside Israel than within. For example, Naaman the Syrian came to faith in the Lord because of his healing (2 Kings 5). These miracles challenged Israel to return to Him so that they could experience such blessings, as promised in their covenant generations earlier, instead of the curses they experienced for their unfaithfulness (Leviticus 26 and Deuteronomy 28).

Certain miracles in the lives of Elijah and Elisha showed that God has the power to sustain His prophets by both natural means in unusual ways, such as by ravens (1 Kings 17:4–6) and by direct angelic help (e.g., 1 Kings 19:5–7). He also used people to meet the needs of His prophets. In one case, He used the least likely of people: a poor Sidonian widow (1 Kings 17:7–16). God helped a student in Elisha's school of prophets recover a borrowed ax head and thus avoid a potentially serious financial problem (2 Kings 6:1–7).[10]

The Restorer through Resurrection

In all of these various interventions, the Lord revealed himself as the great compassionate source of provision for all human need. He also showed that He does signs through His prophets as part of His message of restoration. And although His signs denounce the false prophet, they focus primarily on Him: the One who provides a covenantal, personal relationship with all who will humbly receive it by faith. Genesis through Malachi proclaims that the Lord wants fellowship with people for eternity, and so He personally intervenes as the Deliverer-King to save those who will respond to His gift. God's purpose for His people in this world centers on bringing salvation to everyone (Genesis 12:2–3; Galatians 3:8–9), and so He provides supernatural enabling for this. By signs and wonders the Lord has shown himself to be the all-powerful and benevolent King of the universe who restores all who are willing to fellowship with Him.

The Lord gave the prophets the spiritual interpretations of current events in Israel as signs to reinforce His messages. They constituted fulfillments of the blessings and curses promised in the covenant (Leviticus 26 and Deuteronomy 28), and Moses says that the curses of the covenant will be signs and wonders to Israel of the seriousness of their disobedience (Deuteronomy 28:45–46).

The Lord further sought to motivate Israel by predicting the ultimate events of judgment and salvation that will culminate the history of this world. Jeremiah 30 through 33 offers a prime example of the prophetic promise as he looks beyond Israel's return from captivity, a miracle in itself, to the ultimate spiritual restoration of God's people in the new covenant with forgiveness of sin and new hearts (cf. Ezekiel 36:26–27), including healing for the whole person and community (cf. Isaiah 53:5). Jeremiah says that the Almighty Creator deals with sin through judgment but shows love to those who respond to Him. The saving works of the Exodus have continued to testify of this. God will definitely deal with the current situation, and His word to Jeremiah about future restoration will certainly come to pass. "Nothing is too hard" or "miraculous" for God (32:17). This promise of restoration occurs several times in Jeremiah 30 through 33, concluding with it in 33:26, as well as elsewhere in the Old Testament.

God's greatest miracle will happen when He totally reverses the effects of sin in the lives of people and the effects of the Fall on all creation.[11] This includes the resurrection hope of all believers proclaimed by the whole Bible. In the New Testament the resurrection denotes the ultimate sign and wonder. It confirms and fulfills God's salvation of humanity, His greatest intervention, meeting the ultimate need of the world: deliverance from death for all who will repent and believe.

Ezekiel promises that the nation of Israel will be totally restored in the Promised Land under Davidic leadership as a miracle of resurrection and that this will be a sign to all that the Lord is God (Ezekiel 37). Isaiah, in several places (e.g., 35; 51:3–16; 55:10–13; 60; 62; and 65:8–10,17–25), looks ahead to the ultimate miraculous transformation when the whole creation will be renewed to the harmony of Eden. God will then reestablish His authority completely over all the formerly fallen world. This restoration will forever act as a sign to show the Lord's true greatness (55:13). Thus, one can see the awesome hope of the resurrection implied where David says God will not allow His "Holy One to see decay" (Psalm 16:10)—a verse used in the earliest preaching on the resurrection (see Acts 2:24–32). Daniel 12:2 clarifies that all will be resurrected to either eternal life or eternal shame, which is the ultimate divine intervention and testimony to His sovereignty, holiness, and saving purpose.

Conclusion

The Old Testament teaches that believers may expect signs and wonders because the Lord lovingly rules the universe and intervenes for the eternal good of His creatures. Signs and wonders express and confirm His plan of salvation for the world. God is the ideal King and Father who intervenes to deal with sin, which destroys His creation, and who saves those who will respond to His grace. The Lord is the Mighty Warrior God who conquers all enemies. He offers forgiveness of all sins, totally, being unwaveringly committed to the greatest good for all people. The love of the Creator God for His fallen creatures represents the greatest miracle and central truth of His divine purpose. For those who respond, He provides, guides, and enables them to accomplish His purposes. Signs and wonders refer to the spectacular, direct interventions of God, which bring the response of awe out of people, testifying that He is the incomparable, sovereign God. Prophets, as divine spokespersons, may expect to perform signs and wonders as part of the Lord's message as He directs. God's miraculous acts confirm His Word and should encourage faith by pointing to His love and concern for His people. Such acts often must be understood by faith, recognizing the timing of events in answer to prayer or in accordance with the Lord's pronouncement. Signs and wonders act as reminders of both God's negative dealings with sin as well as His positive blessings for faith. Because He has done such miracles for the good of His people in the past, believers should trust Him for their future, even if it involves a delay or no miracle at all. Ultimately, God will totally restore all creation to complete harmony with himself and resurrect believers to eternal fellowship with himself, and the whole universe will be full of His glory. Truly, His name shall be called "Wonderful."

Endnotes

[1]See J. Rodman Williams, *Renewal Theology* (Grand Rapids: Zondervan Publishing House, 1988), Vol. 1, 141–44, and Wayne Grudem, "Should Christians Expect Miracles Today?" in *The Kingdom and the Power: Are Healing and the Spiritual Gifts Used by Jesus and the Early Church Meant for the Church Today?*, ed. Gary S. Greig and Kevin N. Springer (Ventura, Calif.: Regal Books, 1993), 100–102.

[2]James B. Pritchard, "Motifs of Old Testament Miracles," *Crozer Quarterly* 27 (April 1950), 97. Note that although Pritchard makes good observations on the role of miracles in the text, he believes they are just folk tales.

[3]Victor P. Hamilton, "pala'," in *Theological Wordbook of the Old Testament,* ed. R. Laird Harris, Gleason L. Archer, Jr., and Bruce K. Waltke (Chicago: Moody Press, 1980, 2:723).

[4]J. Alec Motyer, *The Prophecy of Isaiah: An Introduction & Commentary* (Downers Grove, Ill.: InterVarsity Press, 1993), 104.

[5]For a good summary article on prophets and prophecy in the Old Testament, see J. A. Motyer, "Prophecy, Prophets," in *New Bible Dictionary*, 2d ed., ed. J. D. Douglas (Downers Grove, Ill. InterVarsity Press, 1982), 975–83.

[6]For a good summary article on the plagues, see K. A. Kitchen, "Plagues of Egypt," in *New Bible Dictionary*, 2d ed., ed. J. D. Douglas (Downers Grove, Ill. InterVarsity Press, 1982), 943–44.

[7]See the warrior theme below.

[8]See Jeffrey Niehaus, "Old Testament Foundations: Signs and Wonders in Prophetic Ministry and the Substitutionary Atonement of Isaiah 53," in *The Kingdom and the Power*, ed. Gary S. Greig and Kevin N. Springer (Ventura, Calif.: Regal Books, 1993), 42.

[9]For a good discussion of the concept of covenant in the Pentateuch see Elmer A. Martens, *God's Design: A Focus On Old Testament Theology*, 2d ed. (Grand Rapids: Baker Book House, 1994), 74–76.

[10]Pritchard, "Motifs," 107.

[11]Reversal of the Fall does not mean that all physical effects of it are automatically, instantaneously removed for the believer. There is a now/not yet quality to the promises of God until the Second Coming. God provides out of His grace in Christ what He knows is best in this life as our wise parent. Ultimately, when Christ returns, all His promises will be fulfilled (see 1 Corinthians 15:24–27; Hebrews 2:8–9; 1 John 3:2).

3

The Gospel in Action

Benny C. Aker

The world was different then: The first-century, prescientific world believed that all kinds of forces surrounded them and impacted their environment. Evil and mysterious forces caused sickness, threw havoc into the seasons and climate, brought people under the control of fate, and made them do strange things. No wonder they sought to control and manipulate such forces! The first-century Jewish historian Josephus captured the spirit of the age in his history. When writing about wise King Solomon, he drew from the Bible but embellished his account by noting that Solomon's wisdom included various kinds of magical skills and powers, which had passed on to those in Josephus's own day. When a certain Eleazar exorcised a demon in front of the Roman Emperor Vespasian and a host of others, "he put a ring that had a root of one of those sorts mentioned by Solomon to the nostrils of the demoniac, after which he drew out the demon through his nostrils; and when the man fell down immediately, he abjured him to return into him no more, making mention of Solomon, and reciting the incantations which he composed."[1]

The gospel invaded this environment with a solution different from that of the traditional Solomonic one. It contains two major ingredients: (1) the proclaimed Word, which connects the contemporary hearers with the historical once-and-for-all death and resurrection of Jesus, and (2) the deliverance by the Holy Spirit of those who respond by faith. The New Testament, following the Old, calls the latter "signs and wonders." Today evil profoundly holds the world in its grip, and humans desperately need deliverance through signs and wonders—a deliverance that relates to the way God decisively deals with evil as a result of Jesus' mighty works.

New Testament Words

Contemporary literature and speakers, both popular and academic, often indiscriminately use "signs and wonders" for every category of miracle. Scholarly discussions, however, debate this matter and distinguish between them. For instance, Donald A. Carson concludes that a difference exists between "signs and wonders" and "healings."[2] On the other hand, Gary S. Grieg and Kevin N. Springer believe that all the terminology flow together.[3] Let us summarize how the New Testament applies these various words.

The New Testament uses several words for "miracle." The key ones are *dunamis,* "miracle"; *teras,* "wonder"; and *semeion,* "sign." This chapter will focus on these words. When the last two occur together, they signify a special category of miracle. In some contexts, "miracle" can also belong to this special category. The Gospels avoid using the word "sign" or the combination "signs and wonders." "Sign" in Mark 16:17,20 and in the Gospel of John are exceptions. The way they refer to "signs" affirms this conclusion: "Signs and wonders" specifically occurs in evangelistic contexts and manifests God's salvation. Acts, Romans, 2 Corinthians, and Hebrews support this special category. In comparison, the Gospels refer to miracles simply by what they are, healings or exorcisms—the good news of the gospel in action. Acts differs in this by speaking of Jesus as the Gospel. The gospel is the presence, power, and kingdom of Jesus bringing deliverance: Signs and wonders are Kingdom events.

The Book of Acts, some Pauline epistles, and Hebrews 2:4 use signs and wonders in a special way to emphasize the spectacular event of God's presence and mighty power in expelling an evil force from its victim. In Hebrews 2:4, for example, "signs and wonders" occurs with "miracles," connecting the working of the Spirit and the preaching of the gospel: "God witnesses at the same time both in signs and wonders and various kinds of miracles and the Holy Spirit with distributions according to his will."

Here, "miracles" summarize "signs and wonders." "Signs and wonders" and "miracle," when occurring together in the New Testament, are always found in evangelistic and missions contexts. Sometimes "miracle" occurs with the other two words but in doing so does not change its meaning. Twice, Mark 16:17,20 employs "sign" by itself, but there it carries the same meaning as the term "signs and wonders."[4] "Wonder" *(teras),* however, always remains in the plural and with the word "signs."[5]

For the most part, John takes a different direction, using the phrase only in 4:48 and then in a negative way: "Jesus said to him, 'Except you see signs and wonders, you will not believe.'" This Gospel, though, uses "sign" similarly to the way the other Gospels use healings and exorcisms. Signs in John point to Jesus' death, resurrection, ascension, and His nature. Each sign, though different, has a coherent reference. For instance, the changing of water into wine, a nature miracle in John 2, points to the new creation event in the redemptive work of Jesus and in the Church, God's people. Jesus has delivered them from their past sinful nature and its condemnation. Without true faith, unbelievers will not see the saving significance of signs and become true disciples.

When compared to the other three Gospels, John uniquely displays the salvation of God. The book contains no exorcisms—its signs focus on Jesus' death and resurrection as bringing salvation. In the other Gospels, exorcisms, along with healings, display salvation-deliverance.

The Larger Environment of Signs and Wonders

Western culture usually thinks of sin as residing only in individualized human nature. To place signs and wonders in proper perspective, we must explore the larger context of sin and salvation. God is good and everything He made was good, but from the Fall in Genesis 3 onward, humankind has lived in an oppressive environment of evil forces. In the Bible, evil is not just the absence of good or only resident in human nature, but attached to personal beings and forces. Satan and demons oppose God and His people through deception, and work havoc. In the current age, God the Deliverer confronts these evil forces. Yet at the end, God will bring every evil power under submission. To understand the nature of signs and wonders in the present conflict, the three dimensions of sin and salvation require consideration.

First, the internal dimension of sin persists in a person's fallen, sinful nature. Because people received it from Adam corporately, it imprisons all. This requires the creative energy of God in regeneration to free one from its power and bring about a new nature.

Second, the external dimension involves external forces that incarcerate humans and includes demon possession and sickness. These powers also increase the force of temptation.

Third, the social dimension of sin places evil in its larger world of beings, working together in some system or structure. Evil manifests itself corporately in such things as governmental policies, economic theories, systems of justice, and various kinds of social organizations like gangs and syndicated criminal activity. Though some of these can be legitimate, through the combination of evil people and satanic activity, all become corrupt and oppressive, resulting in hunger, starvation, war, slavery, and prejudice.

These three dimensions continue to imprison people, who are forever bound and waiting for a deliverer. At least one of these binds everyone. Two or more bind many. Regardless of the degree to which people are imprisoned, whether by sinful natures, guilt, or demon possession, or as the products of broken families caused by alcoholism or verbal or sexual abuse, God must exercise His power to save and deliver.

Signs and Wonders and the Gospel of the Kingdom

Certain Scripture verses inform us about the three terms "signs," "wonders," and "gospel of the kingdom." On one level, they appear somewhat loosely connected, but upon closer analysis, they prove to be interchangeable and synonymous in many instances.

What does "gospel" mean? To help understand its twofold nature, consider the word "salvation." From an analysis of certain Scripture verses, forensic and deliverance aspects of salvation emerge. Theologically, "forensic" refers to God's gift wherein He declares that the guilty party has received forgiveness and has been justified by faith through Jesus' atoning sacrifice. Another way to understand "forensic" is to compare it with "substitution." Jesus, who did not sin, assumed its penalty when He died for all humankind, transferring their guilt to himself. The forgiven did not participate in this sacrifice. But God acquitted them through faith; hence, they stand in a new relationship and are no longer God's enemies. Thus, "justification" and "reconciliation" are key terms in the meaning of "forensic." It is what God does for us.

Unfortunately, Western Christians have too frequently short circuited the power of forensic justification, since they have left little or no room for signs and wonders as part of the gospel. Certainly, proclamation of the gospel and justification by faith lie at the heart of salvation. The preaching of the gospel releases faith in the person and allows God to forgive sin and transfer the righteousness of Jesus.

Deliverance represents another aspect of the gospel. For example, it is one thing to declare a criminal innocent and quite another to release him from prison. The judge who signed the court document must then send the jailer to release his prisoner. So it is when a sinner comes to God through Jesus in faith and accepts forgiveness. For both aspects of the gospel to be present, something more must happen. That person needs a new nature, perhaps deliverance from demon possession, and a new community.

Isaiah's words in Luke 4:18–19 capture well the forensic and deliverance aspects of the gospel: word and deed. "[God] has anointed me to preach good news to the poor . . . to release the oppressed." The word announces that Jesus has taken care of sin and its consequence. The deed involves signs and wonders, healing, the Spirit's work of regeneration, or, if necessary, casting out a demon. This helps one understand why signs and wonders in the Bible always occur in evangelistic contexts. They are the kingdom of God—the power of Jesus and of the Spirit—delivering people from sin's three dimensions. It is salvation as God's powerful deed delivering the captive from the power of the kingdom of evil. Thus saved, reborn, free from guilt, and possessor of a new relationship with God, one has the Kingdom within.

The gospel in Luke 4:18–19, though, focuses on external and social dimensions of sin and salvation: externally, Jesus heals blind eyes; socially, He frees the prisoners and releases the oppressed. Though deliverance from evil social structures arrives fully when Jesus returns, new social realities can come now in some measure and in some ways. God wishes for His people to live out these realities now. The Lord's Prayer in Matthew 6:9–13 calls for believers to seek God's help in bringing heavenly living to His earthly community and focuses on believers forgiving others as God forgave them.

"Word and deed" represent the norm for biblical Christianity, as reflected in the following texts. Paul in Romans 15:18–19, for example, states: "I dare not speak anything of which Christ did not work through me to bring about the obedience of the Gentiles, in word and deed, in the power of signs and wonders, in the power of the Spirit; so that I have fulfilled the gospel of Christ from Jerusalem even to the surrounding regions of Illyricum."

First, these verses arise from a missions context. Paul, in writing to the Roman church, spoke of his efforts as fulfilling the Great Commission: "The obedience of the Gentiles" comes directly from the Great Commission in Matthew 28:19–20. Paul also wrote particularly about the gospel of Christ as "word and deed" and as "signs and wonders."

Second, he describes the nature of the gospel using two parallel and synonymous elements: "In the power of signs and wonders" parallels "in the power of the Spirit." By putting it this way, Paul connected the Spirit with signs and wonders and informed his readers that the Spirit was the agent behind them. Earlier, he summarized the gospel with "word and deed" and placed them together, making them equal aspects of the gospel. "Word" is only half of the gospel. Though he did not elaborate upon this aspect, he had reference to the verbal proclamation of the crucified and risen Lord. "Deed" comes second, and not by chance. Paul intends the following phrases to modify and amplify "deed," fleshing it out with "the power of signs and wonders" and the parallel "power of the Spirit."

Third, Paul's terms summarize this enterprise with "the works of Christ" and the "gospel of Christ." Jesus works by the Spirit in the gospel through preaching and miraculous activity. As an evangelist preaches, God connects the hearer with Jesus' death and resurrection in history, and through this preaching, the Spirit convicts of sin, awakens faith in hearers to believe (Galatians 3:1–5), and works signs and wonders. Salvation has arrived—the actualization of Jesus' death and resurrection. The end times and the Kingdom have broken into the present age.

Among other texts that show that the gospel consists of proclamation and deed, one bears consideration: Matthew 8:14–17. In

Matthew, this account, though occurring in Mark 1:29–34 and Luke 4:38–41, appears in the middle of a larger section (8:1 through 9:38), recording Jesus' first ministry tour. It immediately follows the Sermon on the Mount but precedes the disciples' mission "to the lost sheep of the house of Israel" in 10:5–42. Here, Jesus presents His method and message of salvation and call to discipleship.[6] In Matthew 8:14–17, several events, happening on the same day, occur in the same paragraph to define the gospel: the healing of Peter's mother-in-law, later healings, and exorcisms. Jesus appealed to Isaiah 53:4 regarding His saving activity: "He took our sicknesses and carried away our illnesses."[7] On the surface, Matthew 8:14–17 appears to be primarily a forensic text; yet upon closer examination, it claims deliverance as its major focus. To Jesus, exorcisms and healings are salvation activities.

Matthew's Gospel does not use the nouns "savior" and "salvation," nor the adjective "saving"; instead, the verb "save" for both healing and the discharge of sins (1:21 and 9:21–22) occurs. The terms Matthew uses for salvation are "healing" and "exorcism." Many passages sum up Jesus' saving work in this manner. In 1:21, Jesus' purpose for coming is to save His people from their sins. Later, when He inaugurated His ministry in 4:23–25, He put forward this saving activity as "teaching," "preaching the gospel of the kingdom," "healing all manner of disease," and "exorcising." Three key ideas emerge: proclamation (word), healings and exorcisms, and the gospel of the Kingdom. Still later, Matthew, in 9:35–38, summarizes Jesus' saving ministry of chapters 8 and 9 and then makes a transition to a fresh chapter (10), which contains teaching for an evangelistic mission. Similar "saving" language also occurs in this paragraph: "teaching," "preaching the gospel of the kingdom," and "healing all kinds of sickness." Furthermore, 9:36 describes sin in social terms.

Scholars and others hold several views about the relationship between "word" and "deed": (1) Miracles (i.e., signs and wonders) confirm, "authenticate," the gospel. However, Scripture does not sustain this view. If it did, "gospel" would then be separated from "word." A Western mind-set owns this view, which reflects a defensive posture. In the rational argumentation and defense of the gospel in this mind-set, "miracle" functions as evidence to validate the deedless word.[8] In response, the gospel needs no confirmation—it needs proclaiming. Miracles are not just confirmatory in nature;[9] they are part of the gospel. (2) Miracles symbolize God's forgiveness but are not really part of the gospel. As a word in language refers to another reality, so a miracle speaks about, stands for, something else. As the word "tree" stands for the real thing, so "miracles" stand for the gospel. (3) Miracles simply illustrate the gospel. As a ritual signifies another level of reality, so miracles illustrate another kind of action. To put it another way, a sermon illustration helps the hearer understand the sermon's point. (4) Miracles are not important. As signs they detract from and thus replace the gospel. People can get so caught up seeking miracles that they seek them rather than the gospel (a view containing assumptions some of the other views hold). (5) Miracles simply accompany the gospel without any connection.[10]

In regard to numbers 3 and 4, the word "sign" *(semeia)* by itself in some contexts does mean symbol or illustration, something that points beyond itself to another reality. But where the words occur together, the contexts mean nothing like this, viewing the gospel rather as both proclamation and deed.

Recognizing Signs and Wonders

How can one recognize signs and wonders when they happen? Must they always be spectacular, divine deeds? Usually, signs and wonders are quite visible or evident in some way. Do certain expectations, however, condition one's understanding of signs and wonders? Could they appear in some other manner outside these expectations?

Since sin and its bondage take many forms, God's deliverance takes appropriate forms in each case. For example, unbelievers have sinful natures that hold them in bondage. When the Spirit regenerates them, they experience signs and wonders, even when exorcism or healing is not necessary. Regeneration is the liberating experience from internal bondage. John's Gospel makes this especially clear (3:3,5): rebirth equals entering the Kingdom. Furthermore, he emphasizes that regeneration, healing, and other miracles (signs) all point to the saving work of Jesus through the regenerating power of the Spirit.[11]

An often misinterpreted text occurs in 1 John 3:4–10, here translated quite literally: "He who habitually practices the sin is of the devil, because the devil sins from the beginning. For this reason [i.e., the works of the devil] the Son of God was manifested: to destroy the works of the devil." "Works of the devil" refers to one's sinful nature (this is what "the sin" above means) and not to demon possession or activity. Such a person, obviously, has not yet been born again. Jesus came to atone for our sins and to send the Spirit to regenerate us. But human nature participates with the devil until it has been regenerated.[12] Significantly, John's writings do not emphasize demonic possession or exorcism.

Conclusion

As we have noted, "signs and wonders" emerges as one of the several categories of miracles in the New Testament. They belong to a special class, describing God's saving activity when people respond by faith to the gospel—they are the necessary events to deliver sinners bound by sin in its various dimensions. New Testament writers, following the Old, combine the words "signs and wonders" to emphasize this activity. This special group arises legitimately from a common classification of meaning from the various contexts and the construction of the term itself.[13] For example, these two words together or in combination with "miracle" emphasize this delivering act.

Some people abused "signs and wonders" in the latter part of the first century. In an environment that readily believed in such, they manipulated pagan and believer alike through "signs and wonders." But their lives had no godly character, only selfish ambition, when leading people astray. For such a trying time, Revelation makes no appeal for signs, wonders, or miracles for prophetic Christian witness or confirmation. In contrast, the book calls for commitment to apostolic doctrine. In fact, those who use signs and wonders for authentication emerge as false prophets who deceive Christians. John, the author of Revelation, calls on Christians in these last days to guard themselves against deception and, if necessary, to die in the face of Satan's coercive threats.[14]

Miracles also confirm some person or the person's ministry. But the New Testament does not pay much positive attention to this category. Usually, to seek confirmation in this manner expresses skepticism or rejection. For instance, Paul, in 1 Corinthians 1:18–31, places Greeks and Jews together when the latter seek a "sign" *(semeia).*[15] In this case, these Jews seek a miracle to affirm one's authority—they thus belong to the "rationalist" school. Only when miracles are absent does one have to appeal to philosophical or apologetical systems. The greatest support for miracles comes when they happen—no confirmation is needed. The true believer does not need miracles to confirm the Bible or preaching. When anyone preaches the gospel in the presence of faith, "signs and wonders," as defined by the New Testament, happen.

If our analysis is correct, signs and wonders differ in at least one sense from the gifts of the Spirit. Paul does not call the charismata "miracles." "Miracles" occur among them (1 Corinthians 12:28–30), serving as a special class of charismata. The term "charismata" describes all the gifts as well as a specific gift among them. In contrast, "miracles" describes only one of the gifts and is not applicable to all the gifts. In 1 Corinthians 12:4,31 "charismata" describes all the gifts, in 12:9,30 a single one (gifts of healings, one gift but plural in form), and in Romans 1:11 an ambiguous one. In fact, Paul does not call gifts of healings "miracles." Miracles, then, must belong to a special class that may even overlap "signs and wonders." Thus, "miracles" may refer to exorcism, something Paul does not include as a gift.

Signs and wonders happen in the forefront of evangelism, where the gospel of the Kingdom works to free people from sin and its complex, imprisoning effects. They also distinguish the church from outsiders. As a result, deliverance and subsequent habitation of God mark the believer more than such valuable things as doctrinal precision, water baptism, and church membership.

Who may do signs and wonders, then? Only God! For it is He who works as believers share the gospel. When one proclaims the gospel, God is there indeed!

Endnotes

[1]*Antiquities of the Jews* 8.2.5 from *The Works of Josephus,* trans. William Whiston, Complete and Unabridged, new updated ed. (Peabody, Mass.: Hendrickson Publishers, 1987). Similar stories occur in the

Babylonia Talmud, the Jewish Rabbah commentaries, and the homileti-cal Pesikta de-Rab Kahana. See the entire work of the *Testament of Solomon.*

[2]Donald A. Carson, "The Purpose of Signs and Wonders in the New Testament," in *Power Religion: The Selling Out of the Evangelical Church?* ed. Michael S. Horton (Chicago: Moody Press, 1992), 89-118.

[3]Gary S. Grieg and Kevin N. Springer, eds., *The Kingdom and the Power: Are Healing and the Spiritual Gifts Used by Jesus and the Early Church Meant for the Church Today?* (Ventura, Calif.: Regal Books, 1993). The literature cited in notes and bibliographies provides a wealth of useful information.

[4]*Semeion* ("sign") occurs far more frequently (about seventy-seven times) than "wonders." A glance through its various contexts reveals a variety of meanings: "miracle," "wonder," and "sign." Most of the time in Matthew, Mark, and Luke, the word carries a negative connotation, especially in Matthew and Mark. In these Gospels, a sign authenticates a role for a messiah-like figure or great prophet and does not signify true faith by observers (Matthew 12:38–42; Mark 8:11–13; Luke 11:29–32). "Sign" in other contexts refers to a portent, a sign in the sky, or it can refer to happenings on the earth which signal the end of the age (e.g., Mark 13:4).

Most of the time, "signs" in Acts occurs with "wonders." Even when alone, as in Acts 8:6, it clearly refers to the same miraculous events as signs and wonders. In the same passage and regarding the impact that Philip had in Samaria, "signs" occurs only with "miracles" (*dunamis*, sin-gular). "Signs," then, as "miracles," and "signs and wonders" in Acts are associated with healing, exorcism, proclamation, and the arrival of the Kingdom. In the Acts 8 account, the gospel's content, the kingdom of God, parallels the name of Jesus (8:12).

[5]"Wonder" occurs in the New Testament sixteen times. Acts 2:19 might be considered an exception: "I will show wonders in the heaven above and signs on the earth below, blood and fire and billows of smoke." Under close examination, however, it fits our conclusion. Acts 2:19 quotes Joel 2:30. The Hebrew text and the Greek translation of the pas-sage contain only "wonders" and that in the first line. In the next line of Joel 2:30, it is omitted. The reader simply supplies the word from the previous line to complete the verse. But Peter's sermon adds the word "signs" instead of allowing "wonders" to be supplied. The passage then reads as follows: "I will show wonders in heaven above and signs on the earth below." The third line, which specifies what these signs will be, assumes the same meaning for both "wonders" and "signs."

[6]This text, then, gives us entry into the worldview of Jesus and, there-fore, into the backgrounds of Mark and Luke.

[7]Isaiah 53:4 only occurs in Matthew. Here, Matthew's text of this pas-sage follows the general sense of the Hebrew; however, it does not follow

the Septuagint (Greek) translation. Matthew's citation through his context points more sharply to Jesus' saving activity as exorcisms and healings than either the Hebrew or Greek.

⁸A defensive posture regarding miracles comes through in many ways. Courses on apologetics have been taught in many Evangelical schools over the years, although this emphasis has declined somewhat. Occasionaly books on apologetics are still published: for example, Norman L. Geisler's *Miracles and the Modern Mind: A Defense of Biblical Miracles* (Grand Rapids: Baker Book House, 1992). On page 97, Geisler states clearly that both Old and New Testament miracles serve a confirmatory purpose. Fundamentalists and some conservative evangelicals have roots in the older liberal/conservative debate. Interestingly enough, while believing that miracles occurred in Bible times, they partially assume the same posture as that of the old liberals. They are as rational as the rest. As a result, preaching and theological literature mirror a defensive posture.

⁹One category of miracles does serve a confirmatory function, although not in the modern, Western sense. Acts 2:22 does not necessarily contain a reference to "confirmation"—another interpretation is possible. In part, the verse reads: "Jesus the Nazarene, a man set forth by God for you in miracles, signs, and wonders. . . ." I translate the relevant word, *apodedeigmenon,* as "set forth." The word can also mean "accredited" as in the NIV.

¹⁰For example, see the views expressed in Horton, *Power Religion;* Charles H. Kraft, *Christianity with Power: Your Worldview and Your Experience of the Supernatural* (Ann Arbor, Mich.: Servant Publications, 1989); Graham H. Twelftree, *Jesus the Exorcist: A Contribution to the Study of the Historical Jesus* (Tübingen, W. Germany: J. C. B. Mohr, 1993; reprint, Peabody, Mass.: Hendrickson Publishers, n.d.).

¹¹The information in this paragraph does expand the traditional definition of "signs and wonders," but when examining John (and the rest of the New Testament), surprises often emerge. On the other hand, this definition simultaneously narrows and excludes human responses to divine activity in the personality such as shaking, jerking, and laughing. This makes no value judgment on such responses—it only excludes them from among "signs and wonders" in the biblical sense.

¹²In 1 John this does not refer to eradication of the possibility to sin. John, like Paul, refers to one's liberation from the bondage of the unregenerate nature.

¹³This is called a hendiadys. When two nouns are connected by "and," the second one acts as an adjective, thus emphasizing in some way the idea. The two together, then, present a single, heightened meaning.

¹⁴See, for example, Revelation 13:10 for encouragement and verses 13 to 18 for the beast's power and authority and its display of signs and

wonders. Even though Revelation plays down signs and wonders, one should not look down upon them. More than likely real signs and wonders by Christian evangelists continued during this period, but the miraculous, broadly understood and undifferentiated, so commonly taken for granted in this environment became the confirming "wonder" in the contest for power. The New Testament differentiated among the miraculous activities and gave vastly different reasons for them.

[15]See also Matthew 12:38–42 and Luke 11:29–32 where Jesus calls those who seek signs a wicked generation.

4

The Radical Strategy

Gary B. McGee

The air filled with expectancy when the healing line formed and a little boy born without a hip socket approached the evangelist for prayer. Laying hands on him, the evangelist prayed for healing. When the miracle occurred, the crowd stood and surged forward. Those who had been unable to walk suddenly stood as well and began to walk. Crutches were thrown down. People with seeing and hearing impairments testified to healing and all praised God. This story sounds like it came from the Book of Acts. Actually, it happened nineteen centuries after the Day of Pentecost at Oral Roberts's Jacksonville, Florida, campaign in 1952.[1]

Many Christians today long to see this kind of spiritual power: the signs and wonders performed by Jesus and the apostles (Acts 2:22; 5:12) and promised to all (John 14:12). Christianity has experienced several dramatic shifts in this century, including the extraordinary emphasis currently placed on the ministry of the Holy Spirit. Although some may believe that the Spirit's power has only now been fully restored after nearly two thousand years, that is not the case.

Miracles after the Apostles

Supernatural phenomena, notably miracles as well as the gifts of the Holy Spirit, continued in sectors of the Church long after the time of the apostles. The fourth-century "desert father"

Antony of Egypt became legendary for his spiritual warfare with demons. At about the same time, Nino, a slave girl taken captive to the Caucasus region of Georgia, prayed for the healing of a member of the royal family. The miracle then led to the nation's conversion. Miracle stories appeared in the Medieval Era as well, although they often became clouded with fantastic claims.

With the coming of the Protestant Reformation (1500 through 1650), Protestant and Catholic theologians clashed over such issues as the nature of sin, justification by faith, the sacraments, and the authority of Scripture. By teaching on the priesthood of all believers, Martin Luther, Huldrych Zwingli, and John Calvin disavowed the Catholic doctrine of the communion of Mary and the saints, thereby dismissing the value set on the saints, holy relics, shrines, pilgrimages, and the miracle stories that developed around them.

Later in the sixteenth and seventeenth centuries, Lutheran and Reformed theologians returned to the late medieval practice of using philosophical reasoning, chiefly the form of logic cultivated by Aristotle, to help build doctrine. The fruits of their labors can be seen in conservative Protestant theology today and in tomes of dogmatic theology that probe every crevice of doctrine. Nonetheless, the arid discussions of Protestant orthodoxy took place at the very time when piety had declined in the churches. In part, defending doctrine led theologians to fear that subjective religious experience would scuttle the Bible's authority; hence, they nurtured the religion of the head more than the religion of the heart.

Doubts versus Heartfelt Salvation

Reason's assault on Scripture and doctrine began in the eighteenth century, the same period that evangelical awakenings flourished in Germany, England, and the United States. The Enlightenment, or Age of Reason, aimed its skepticism at anything considered miraculous. Humankind had only now come of age, thanks to rational thinking's liberation from superstition. Though much Enlightenment philosophy undermined traditional Christian beliefs, the value set on scientific experiment influenced the theology of evangelical revivalists: Experiment, better described in this context as "experience," when related to heartfelt conversion dismissed the question of whether one had been predestined to salvation. John and Charles Wesley in England and the later American revivalist Charles G. Finney, along with others, highlighted the personal assurance of redemption. In turn, this provided a simple and comforting conviction of the Christian faith's truthfulness in an atmosphere of skepticism.

Experiential piety, however, unintentionally encouraged various manifestations in revival services and camp meetings: believers falling down (referred to today as being slain in the Spirit or resting in the Spirit), laughing, weeping, shouting, barking, and dancing. The popular piety of most American Christians included the possibility of miracles, although theologians contended that miracles had ended with the apostolic period in practice, if not in theory. Evangelists who daringly prayed for the sick felt the sting of ridicule, despite reports of healings in their services. Because seekers frequently fell prostrate in Maria B. Woodworth-Etter's meetings, critics dubbed this itinerant preacher the "Trance Evangelist."

It seems that as a rule, missionaries, both Protestant and Roman Catholic, doubted the availability of miracles. At the 1860 international missions conference in Liverpool, England, comparing modern missionaries to the apostles, Frederick Trestrail, the secretary of the Baptist Missionary Society, fluttering above the constraints of logic, triumphantly noted: "Divest the Apostles of miraculous power . . . and you have the *modern missionary,* a true successor of the Apostles."[2] In place of supernatural demonstrations of power, Western missionaries confidently shared the blessings of their "higher" civilization to further the gospel. For most Christians, the postmillennial calendar with its optimism of Christianizing society nurtured the hope that after a lengthy period of progress, Christ would return. Nevertheless, the number of converts proved meager (only 3.6 million communicants and adherents by 1906) when compared to the enormous investment of personnel and monies by Western mission agencies.

The Radical Strategy

The nineteenth century introduced an age of awakenings. One of the most significant, the great prayer revival, started just before the American Civil War, in 1858. It soon spread to Canada, Northern Ireland (Ulster), Wales, England, South Africa, and South India. Startled Presbyterians in Northern Ireland observed unusual happenings: especially noted was that hundreds of people fell to the ground, stricken or prostrated by God's power, under intense conviction of sin. Even more surprising, followers of John Christian Aroolappen, the South Indian Christian, spoke in tongues, prophesied, recounted visions, fell prostrate, prayed for the sick, helped the poor, and evangelized non-Christians. The revival there also gave prominence to women, a notable feature in Pentecostal renewals (Joel 2:28–29; Acts 21:9).[3] Years later, in another part of the world and unrelated to the prayer revival, missionary Johannes Warneck recorded that the Indonesian Christian community had increased after the appearance of similar Pentecostal phenomena: dreams, visions, signs in the heavens, and several instances where missionaries unwittingly drank poison given by their enemies and remained unharmed (Joel 2:28–31; Mark 16:18).[4]

Believers who contended that supernatural signs should follow the preaching of the gospel (Mark 16:17–18) helped set the stage for the "radical strategy": an apocalyptic scenario of divine intervention in signs and wonders to ensure that every tribe and nation would hear the gospel in the last days (Matthew 24:14; Acts 1:8).[5] Those who reflected on the availability of miracles included Anthony Norris Groves (Brethren missionary to India), Thomas Erskine (Scottish lay theologian), Edward Irving (leader of a Pentecostal movement in England), and Horace Bushnell (an American theologian).[6] This list, however, would be incomplete without the name of George Müller, a well-known philanthropist whose expectant faith for God's provision at his orphan homes in Bristol, England, modeled the idealized "faith life" for many Christians. Although not remembered for advocating signs and wonders, his perspective on faith helped lay the theoretical basis.

Why did Christians become interested in miraculous power? First, a wide spectrum of Protestants, both at home and on the mission fields, prayed through the century for the outpouring of the Spirit according to Joel's prophecy (2:28–32). Effective evangelism and reforming society's evils (e.g., slavery, drunkenness, political corruption) required divine enablement.

The slow development of medical science and the cries of the terminally ill also prompted Christians (usually those linked to the Holiness movement) to examine scriptural promises of healing (e.g., Isaiah 53:4–5; James 5:13–16). Testimonies of healing from the ministries of Dorothea Trudel (Switzerland) and Johann Christoph Blumhardt (Germany) influenced the American healing movement, including Charles C. Cullis, A. B. Simpson, A. J. Gordon, John Alexander Dowie, and Maria B. Woodworth-Etter.

Finally, after the Civil War many evangelicals began to reassess human progress. On the premillennial scoreboard of prophetic fulfillment, the world would go from bad to worse before Christ's return. With the end of the century nearing, with an arms race heating up between the major powers, with increasing political and military tensions ("wars and rumors of wars"), and with Zionists calling for a Jewish homeland in Palestine, numerous believers speculated that Christ would return by 1900 or thereabouts. With deepening concern, keen observers of the missions scene wondered how the Great Commission could be accomplished in such a short time.

Expecting Signs and Wonders

More than anyone else after the mid-nineteenth century, A. B. Simpson, the former Presbyterian minister who founded the Christian and Missionary Alliance, put theory into action by encouraging the faithful to trust God for miracles. Along with others, he believed that God would heal the sick, and even considered it possible that the Spirit might confer known languages (i.e., speaking in tongues) to expedite preaching to every tribe and nation. Opponents called such notions absurd and irresponsible. Fanny Guinness, editor of a missionary monthly, *The Regions Beyond,* sniffed that for the heathen, "miracles cannot enlighten their dark minds, or soften their hard hearts. . . . Our aim is to enlighten, not to astonish."[7] She didn't foresee that healings and "power encounters" could break evil's stranglehold on non-Christians. Guinness and most Western Christians paid scant attention to the similarities between native worldviews encountered on mission fields and those encountered within the New Testament. Radical evangelicals, however, increasingly discerned the kinship. To Simpson, "the plan of the Lord [is] to pour out His Spirit not only in the ordinary, but also in the extraordinary gifts and operations of His power . . . as His people press forward to claim the evangelization of the entire world."[8]

Sometimes this method worked better in theory, however, than in practice. In 1890, missionaries from Topeka, Kansas, influenced by Simpson, arrived in Sierra Leone confident of biblical promises of healing and Pentecostal tongues for gospel preaching. After discovering their need to learn the native dialect, they persevered, but three died from malaria, having refused to take quinine.[9]

Raising Expectations

Clearly this revolutionary concept emerged from those few, like Simpson and the Kansas missionaries, who believed that God would provide supernatural aid. One radical, Frank W. Sandford, founded a community and the Holy Ghost and Us Bible School in Shiloh, Maine, to prepare an elite band of end-times missionaries. Affirming signs and wonders, he called his organization the World's Evangelization Crusade on Apostolic Principles.[10] Although he apparently did not speak in tongues himself, others did. With connections to Sandford's enterprise, Walter S. and Frances Black and Jennie Glassey testified to Spirit baptism and receiving new languages during an 1895 revival in St. Louis, Missouri. In view of their newfound ability, Walter Black looked at contemporary mission endeavors and crowed that neither "20,000 nor 100,000 missionaries of the common sanctified type will [ever] evangelize this globe." Instead, God's church needed to operate "with purely Holy Ghost machinery." Glassey claimed having received several African dialects: Hausa, Kru, Khoominar, and later the "Chinese language." Before long, they too headed for Sierra Leone.[11]

A Midwestern Holiness preacher, Charles F. Parham, took special interest in the missionary implications of Glassey's testimony. In April 1900, he announced that a Brother and Sister Hamaker resided at his Topeka, Kansas, faith home "to labor for Jesus until He gives them an heathen tongue, and then they will proceed to the missionary field."[12] During the summer, Parham visited Shiloh, where he heard speaking in tongues for the first time. Convinced that the gift of languages offered the key to a

Spirit-empowered ministry in signs and wonders, Parham and his students at Bethel Bible School prayed in January 1901 for the fulfillment of Joel's prophecy. Participants testified, as others did later at the Azusa Street revival (1906 through 1909) in Los Angeles, and elsewhere, that God had given them the languages of the world. They could now bypass language school and leave immediately for the mission fields.[13] For Pentecostals, this resolved the long-standing question in holiness circles about the evidence of Spirit baptism. In addition, social and cultural factors influenced the emergence of Pentecostalism (also known as the Apostolic Faith or Latter Rain movement).

The language proposal severely tested the credulity of other radical evangelicals, but it retained an empirical tinge: languages could be verified. Yet evidence that Pentecostals did indeed preach in new languages proved difficult to find. By late 1906 and 1907, though still believing that tongues signified human languages or those of angels (1 Corinthians 13:1), Pentecostals began to view it as glossolalia (i.e., unknown tongues to speaker and hearer). Hence, praying in tongues, an exercise that Parham dismissed, brought empowerment through worship and intercession in the Spirit.

Critics, however, branded glossolalia as nonsense. What's more, Pentecostals had crossed into the realm of the irrational and perhaps the satanic. Evangelical Christians were already becoming aware of the encroachment of theosophy, Christian Science, and spiritualism. Not only did speaking in tongues occur among spiritualists, but among Mormons as well. If these threats failed to rattle the faithful, John L. Nevius, a Presbyterian missionary, did—by telling of exorcisms in China where demons had spoken in tongues.[14]

Most Pentecostals taught that every Christian should seek Spirit baptism with tongues and then the gifts of the Spirit. In evangelism, they prioritized seeking for spectacular displays of divine power: signs and wonders, divine healing, and deliverance from sinful habits and satanic bondage. For example, on the home front, differences between evangelical and Pentecostal tactics in evangelism become quickly apparent when one compares the early twentieth-century ministries of Billy Sunday and Aimee Semple McPherson. In 1912, with the support of the ministerial alliance, Billy Sunday held an evangelistic campaign in

Canton, Ohio, preceded by months of planning, construction of a wooden tabernacle, and training of a six-hundred-voice choir. Thousands attended the services and, as Sunday said, "hit the sawdust trail" (variously meaning to commit one's life to Christ, be a good American, or take the pledge to not consume liquor). Nine years later, Aimee Semple McPherson arrived with almost no preparation. Permitted to use the civic auditorium, she began preaching and praying for the sick. Newspaper headlines immediately screamed: "Cripples Are Cured When Woman Evangelist Prays," "Sick of Soul and Body Are Relieved," and "Two Hundred Men Answer Call for Prayer." Seekers jammed the meetings nightly and several thousand professed salvation. McPherson attributed the results to "preaching . . . the great 'I Am' instead of the great 'I Was' "—asserting that Jesus would do today what He had done for the sick and needy during His earthly ministry.[15] Her evangelistic campaigns, combined with those of other Pentecostal evangelists (e.g., Raymond T. Richey, Charles S. Price) led to the founding of thousands of congregations. Pentecostals quickly became adept at planning, but they maintained that well-oiled campaign techniques could never substitute for demonstrations of supernatural power.

Reformulating the strategy to include tongues and spiritual gifts, however, occasionally led to unusual claims: Some predicted earthquakes, others announced that God had appointed them as apostles. Pentecostals soon became wary of such assertions and, more importantly, realized that signs and wonders was not the sole means for winning the world to Christ. Church planting required discipling converts, training leaders, and even preparing Bible translations.

At the same time, expectancy of supernatural interventions continued among less radical evangelicals. Healings, exorcisms, and other extraordinary happenings occurred in the ministries of pastors, evangelists, and missionaries in the Christian and Missionary Alliance, the National Holiness Missionary Society (later the World Gospel Mission), the Church of the Nazarene, and the Missionary Church Association, among others.[16] Although less well known, this has been true across a still broader spectrum of evangelical Christians (e.g., Elijah Bingham, Dick Hillis, Corrie ten Boom, James M. Hickson, and members of the Order of St. Luke [interdenominational]).[17] Yet polemical controversy over tongues and healing evangelists kept many fundamentalists and evangelicals from seeking signs and wonders.

Crisis and Controversy

By the 1940s, Pentecostals started coming out of sectarian isolation to identify with conservative evangelicals. But in the estimation of some, the power of early Pentecostalism had waned. Fears that denominational structures, theological education, and newfound respectability quenched the freedom of the Spirit prompted another revival, the *"New Order* of the Latter Rain" (my emphasis). This divided those who, on the one hand, said the Pentecostal movement's theology and practice had matured and those who, on the other hand, championed a more open-ended view of the Spirit's gifts and workings, one without denominational and sometimes even hermeneutical constraint.

Immediately controversy erupted: Denominational Pentecostal leaders, especially those in the Assemblies of God, found unacceptable the impartation of spiritual gifts through the laying on of hands, restoration of the offices of apostle and prophet, prophecies of guidance given to individuals, and insistence that the Spirit would dispense languages to missionaries.[18] Opinions on the genuineness of the revival varied considerably, revealing a growing gap between "establishment" and "grassroots," or "folk," Pentecostals. Not wishing to repeat what they perceived as mistakes of their past, Pentecostal leaders who saw their institutions threatened by a new movement with questionable teachings distanced themselves from it and in certain cases condemned it.

If the Latter Rain movement proved divisive, the closely related healing movement of the late 1940s and 1950s fostered a measure of unity. Pentecostals of every stripe gathered in tents and auditoriums to see the power and demonstration of the Holy Spirit. Though some healing evangelists exaggerated claims and had questionable lifestyles, their campaigns produced thousands of converts. Through the ministries of William Branham, Oral Roberts, Jack Coe, Gordon Lindsay, and many more, believers professed faith for seemingly impossible problems. Overseas campaigns impacted church growth as well. Perhaps the most spectacular campaign took place in Buenos Aires, Argentina, in

1954, and was led by Tommy Hicks. With an aggregate attendance of nearly two million people, and driven by testimonies of notable healings and deliverances, it resulted in a major breakthrough for Protestantism there.[19]

At the same time, "evangelicalization" of doctrine, worship, and practice escalated in the Assemblies of God and other Pentecostal denominations.[20] Precision in exegesis and doctrine, concern for doctrinal uniformity, and fears of Latter-Rain excesses created uneasiness among establishment Pentecostals, and with some justification. Not surprisingly, their hesitations came again to the fore when the charismatic renewal arose in the 1960s and 1970s and Latter Rain features reappeared in some quarters. Nevertheless, many grassroots Pentecostal ministers and laypersons attended charismatic prayer meetings and avidly read the books of well-known leaders (e.g., Dennis Bennett, Bob Mumford, Kenneth Hagin, John and Elizabeth Sherrill, Pat Robertson, and Francis MacNutt) who emphasized the power of God in Christian living. Generally speaking, charismatics often became more overtly supernaturalistic and prayed in tongues more than their Pentecostal brothers and sisters.

The debate reached a new level of intensity after 1980 with the rise of conservative evangelical charismatics (so-called Third Wavers). Shying away from identification with classical Pentecostals and other charismatics, leaders such as Charles Kraft, C. Peter Wagner, and John Wimber have reformulated the radical strategy with new insights on how to minister in the Spirit's power. Perhaps the most striking teaching has been the insistence that before effective evangelism can be accomplished, territorial demons governing regions of the world must be bound (Matthew 12:29; 18:18).[21]

Reflections

In this brief analysis of signs and wonders in the history of evangelism, four observations stand out.

First, sizable church growth has resulted from miracles and power encounters in non-Western societies, although other crucial factors have been involved. The remarkable crusades of Carlos Annacondia in Argentina and Reinhard Bonnke in Africa and the ministry of David Yonggi Cho in Korea, all distinguished by signs and wonders, have had far-reaching effects. The same has been true of charismatic Lutherans in Ethiopia and the global missionary witness of Pentecostal and charismatic congregations in Singapore.

Unfortunately, problems of various kinds have surfaced when notions of signs and wonders drift from biblical moorings: The quest for power supersedes holiness of character, and practitioners contend that miracles are the chief stimulus for church growth. Affirming belief in miracles does not require suspending judgment; Christians should always test everything (1 Thessalonians 5:21).

A second observation is that differences exist between miracles and human responses. Resting in the Spirit, laughter, and dancing represent reactions to the Spirit's presence and power; they also reflect a person's cultural background, social standing, emotional makeup, and need at the moment. While not without challenges, they may have positive dimensions. During the awakening that swept through mission stations in India in 1905, missionaries who rebuked Indian believers for their emotionalism stopped the moving of the Spirit. But those who recognized the revival's integrity and looked charitably on cross-cultural differences saw revival fires blaze brightly.

Third, strategies, paradigms, and patterns depict human attempts to understand and manage the heavenly agenda. All those who pursue the radical strategy, however, inevitably face the frustration of why miracles may not happen as anticipated: Mystery often shrouds the divine will. God's Word bears fruit with or without visible miracles (e.g., physical healings), and He also works providentially in human affairs. In recent years, Pentecostals and charismatics, recognizing the connection of signs and wonders with the advancing kingdom of God (e.g., Matthew 4:23), have made vital progress in understanding the nature and role of miracles.[22]

The fourth observation is that miracles have usually occurred where believers have expected God to heal and deliver. The contrast between the campaigns of Sunday and McPherson can still be seen in the ministries of such evangelists as Billy Graham and Reinhard Bonnke. Graham neither prays for the sick nor exorcises demons in his services. Bonnke, on the other hand, both preaches and prays for signs and wonders to confirm the gospel message, offering healing to body, soul, and spirit. Both constitute valid and complementary methods of evangelism with neither standing above critique.

In perhaps their greatest contribution to modern Christianity, apart from the church growth that has ensued, those who pursue the radical strategy have moved the anticipation of divine power from the periphery of the Christian world mission to a position at the center. This development has challenged Christians everywhere to look again at the Spirit's work in Church and mission.

If Oral Roberts and his audience had not expected a miracle at the Jacksonville campaign, the service would probably have ended on time . . . as usual.

Endnotes

[1]David Edwin Harrell, Jr., *Oral Roberts: An American Life* (San Francisco: Harper & Row, Publishers, 1985), 106.

[2]Frederick Trestrail, "On Native Churches," *Conference on Missions Held in 1860 at Liverpool* (London: James Nisbet & Co., 1860), 279.

[3]See G. H. Lang, ed., *The History and Diaries of an Indian Christian* (London: Thynne & Co., 1939).

[4]Johannes Warneck, *The Living Christ and Dying Heathenism*, 3d ed. (New York: Fleming H. Revell Co., n.d.), 175–182.

[5]For a more detailed discussion, see my " 'Power From On High': A Historical Perspective on the Radical Strategy in Missions" in *Pentecostalism in Contexts: Essays Presented to William W. Menzies on the Occasion of His Sixty-Fifth Birthday,* ed. Robert P. Menzies and Wonsuk Ma (forthcoming).

[6]See G. H. Lang, *Anthony Norris Groves* (London: Thynne & Co., 1939); C. Gordon Strachan, *The Pentecostal Theology of Edward Irving* (London: Darton, Longman & Todd, 1973); Thomas Erskine, *The Supernatural Gifts of the Spirit,* ed. R. Kelso Carter (Philadelphia: Office of "Words of Faith," 1883); Horace Bushnell, *Nature and the Supernatural* (New York: Charles Scribner, 1858), 446–528.

[7]Mrs. H. Grattin [Fanny] Guinness, "Missionaries According to Matt. X. A Critique," *Regions Beyond* (April 1889): 110.

[8]A. B. Simpson, "Connection Between Supernatural Gifts and the World's Evangelization," *Christian Alliance and Missionary Weekly,* October 7 & 14, 1892, 226.

[9]Mrs. H. Grattin Guinness, "Faith-Healing and Missions," *The Regions Beyond,* January 1891, 31.

[10]Frank W. Sandford, *Seven Years with God* (Mount Vernon, N.H.: The Kingdom Press, 1957), 111–132.

[11]"'Tongues of Fire.' 'Other Tongues.'," *Tongues of Fire,* April 15, 1896, 58–59.

[12]Untitled news note, *Apostolic Faith* (Topeka, Kan.), April 1, 1900, 7.

[13]"Parham's New Religion Practiced at 'Stone's Folly,'" *Kansas City Times,* January 27, 1901, 55.

[14]John L. Nevius, *Demon Possession and Allied Themes* (New York: Fleming H. Revell Co., 1896), 46–47, 58–59.

[15]Aimee Semple McPherson, *This Is That* (Los Angeles: Echo Park Evangelistic Association, 1923), 378.

[16]E.g., Charles W. Nienkirchen, *A. B. Simpson and the Pentecostal Movement* (Peabody, Mass.: Hendrickson Publishers, 1992), 122–128; W. W. Cary, *Story of the National Holiness Missionary Society,* 2d ed. (Chicago: National Holiness Missionary Society, 1941), 48, 189; Russell V. DeLong and Mendell Taylor, *Fifty Years of Nazarene Missions,* Vol. II: History of the Fields (Kansas City, Mo.: Beacon Hill Press, 1955), 291–292, 294; J. A. Ringenberg, *Jesus the Healer* (Fort Wayne, Ind.: Missionary Church Association, 1947), 76.

[17]E.g., *Demon Experiences in Many Lands* (Chicago: Moody Press, 1960), 11–14, 37–40; also James M. Hickson, *Heal the Sick* (New York: E. P. Dutton and Co., n.d.); Corrie ten Boom, *Defeated Enemies* (Fort Washington, Penn.: Christian Literature Crusade, 1963).

[18]See Richard M. Riss, *Latter Rain* (Mississauga, Ont.: Honeycomb Visual Productions, 1987).

[19]Arno W. Enns, *Man, Milieu and Mission in Argentina* (Grand Rapids: William B. Eerdmans Publishing Co., 1971), 76–78.

[20]Russell P. Spittler, "Are Pentecostals and Charismatics Fundamentalists? A Review of American Uses of These Categories," in *Charismatic Christianity as a Global Culture,* ed. Karla Poewe (Columbia, S.C.: University of South Carolina Press, 1994), 103–116.

[21]See C. Peter Wagner, *Warfare Prayer* (Ventura, Calif.: Regal Books, 1992).

[22]E.g., Gordon D. Fee, "The Kingdom of God and the Church's Global Mission," in *Called & Empowered: Global Mission in Pentecostal Perspective,* ed. Murray W. Dempster, Byron D. Klaus, and Douglas Petersen (Peabody, Mass.: Hendrickson Publishers, 1991), 7–21.

5

Preparation for Signs and Wonders

R. Paul and Wardine Wood

Oppressive heat, clouds of dust, and persistent gnats marked another hot Sunday morning in the village of Tabligbo, Togo, West Africa, in October 1979. Seated underneath a canopy of woven branches and standing well beyond its borders, a mass of people worshiped exuberantly. A circuit rider and his five village congregations had joined us for this special service. No fans, microphones, or piano graced the occasion, but the air was charged as believers mingled their hearts and voices in worship. They sang for a full hour, accompanied by drums, small percussion instruments of gourds and beads, and syncopated clapping. Looking heavenward and swaying rhythmically to the music, the congregation appeared to be in one mind and one accord. The passing hours and relentless heat appeared to have little effect. Nothing mattered but giving God praise and glory.

At the height of the worship, an elder, who looked vaguely familiar to us, stood and began to dance down the aisle toward the platform. The other elders followed. Eleven men danced their way to the front of the worshipers and continued to dance in a circular path defined by the leader. He bent down, leaped high in the air, spun and kicked, all to the rhythm of the music and without lessening the sense of order and worship. God allowed two American missionary professors to witness a demonstration of how David must have "danced before the Lord" (2 Sam. 6:14).

Puzzled, Paul leaned toward the pastor, seated to his left, and asked, "Pastor, have I met that brother before?" With a big smile he said, "Yes, that is the man we prayed for yesterday!" The day before, the two of us, along with a resident missionary couple and the young pastor, had spent the afternoon in pastoral visitation. Accustomed to making his rounds on a bicycle, the pastor had thoroughly enjoyed the mission's car whisking us from village to village. As we approached the last one on his circuit, he explained that the elder and his family—the only Christians in the village—had not been able to come to services for several weeks. He suffered from arthritis that caused swelling of the joints; the constant pain made his movement almost unbearable.

As we sat outside the elder's thatch-covered mud hut, curious villagers gathered. We shared God's Word with him and expressed our desire to pray for his healing. With expectation written on every line of his wrinkled face, he led us into his hut and sat down on a stool. The five of us prayed fervently and asked God for His power to heal this elder for His name's sake; outside many of the villagers jeered, amused by the white man's attempt at magic. When we drove away, we had witnessed no change.

Now, this brother was dancing before the Lord with movements of a young athlete. After the service that morning, Paul talked with him and learned the rest of the story. The man had gone to bed Saturday night, had slept well, and had awakened Sunday morning able to move without pain. Running outside his hut, he proclaimed the good news to his neighbors. To their amazement this man who had barely been able to take a step was completely well. The elder pranced, skipped, and praised God as he led the entire village like a pied piper on the six-mile trek to the meeting in Tabligbo.

In the gospel we have both preaching and deed—"signs and wonders"—which explains why signs and wonders in the New Testament always carry evangelistic implications. The miraculous takes place at the cutting edge of evangelism, where the gospel of God's kingdom is at work freeing people from the bondage of sin and triumphing over satanic opposition. Clearly the healing of the elder in Tabligbo had two purposes: It alleviated the suffering of a believer (James 5:14–15), and it served as a sign to nonbelievers. The people of his village had seen the gospel of Jesus Christ before they heard it proclaimed by a missionary. The healing of the elder and the proclamation of the

Word were two events in a "power encounter" between the kingdom of God and the kingdom of Satan, resulting in many lives being set free.

Are signs and wonders restricted to remote areas of the world, or can they be expected to occur in any cultural context? Our premise is that signs and wonders have relevance for today and can happen in any culture.[1] Can Christians participate in the miraculous? How does one's worldview affect one's readiness for signs and wonders? How can Christians prepare for signs and wonders? This chapter explores these issues and suggests answers to these questions.

Participation versus Manipulation

Throughout the course of church history, human beings have sought to control their lives and relegate God to a subservient role. When the roles of God and human beings are reversed, carnality dominates. In the story of Simon the sorcerer, Simon went to Peter and John to purchase the power to impart the Holy Spirit by the laying on of hands, seeing its potential for his self-serving ambitions. Recognizing Simon's motives, Peter rebuked him (Acts 8:17–24).

The Old Testament presents a lofty view of God. Isaiah saw Him "high and lifted up" (Isaiah 6:1, KJV). The Psalms resound with praise to the Creator, Redeemer, and Lord. Ezekiel refers to God as "Sovereign Lord," indicating His complete freedom from human control and emphasizing His position of mastery. Malachi 3:6 declares God's immutability—His unchangeableness: "I the Lord do not change." Each writer sees God as holy, sovereign, and unchangeable.

Yet the supernatural happenings recorded in Scripture clearly indicate that God effects change in human circumstances. A man with leprosy came to Jesus and said, " 'Lord, if you are willing, you can make me clean.' Jesus . . . touched the man. 'I am willing,' he said. 'Be clean!' " (Matthew 8:2–3). In the Sermon on the Mount, Jesus emphasized the readiness of God to intervene in the lives of His children: "How much more will your Father in heaven give good gifts to those who ask him!" (Matthew 7:11).

Believers can influence the activity of God but must not attempt to manipulate Him. The creature does not control the

Creator. Many references in the Old Testament document God's blessings on His people for their obedience and His judgment for their disobedience. An abundance of promises in the Bible are predicated upon meeting certain conditions. For example, Jesus promised, " 'Give, and it will be given to you. A good measure, pressed down, shaken together and running over, will be poured into your lap' " (Luke 6:38). This indicates that the receiving of material blessings is usually based on meeting God's condition of giving. When believers knowingly fail to meet the requirements that God has established, they have no right to expect Him to fulfill the promise. In some situations, failure can risk a stinging rebuke, such as God gave to Israel (Isaiah 1:10–17). Christians should eagerly desire and anticipate God's miraculous intervention in their lives and circumstances. When men and women covenant with God in relationship, obedience, and petition, they partner with Him in the interest of His creation.

The Bible shows that human engagement with God demands preparation, evidenced by the Abrahamic covenant, the Exodus, the Mosaic covenant, and the requirements for the Church as the "bride of Christ." It follows that a Holy God requires believers to prepare for the manifestation of His presence and power. Many of God's commands recorded in the Bible seem mundane, tedious, e.g., the Levitical laws, tempting one to ignore the ordinary commands of God and focus on His spectacular manifestations—the cloud, the pillar of fire, the voice, or the Shekinah. However, the ordinary can be of extraordinary significance to God.

What should be the Christian's approach to participation in the miraculous? We do not believe in following fixed procedures, nor that God works the miraculous only when individuals meet all His requirements. Scripture and Church history record incidents of God's extraordinary involvement with individuals that can be explained only as sovereign acts.

How individuals view the supernatural world determines their response to the miraculous. For example, if one believes that God created the universe, put natural laws in motion, then abandoned the universe to the control of those laws, that person is unlikely to expect or pray for divine intervention in the circumstances of life. Conversely, the person who sees the involvement of spirit beings in every aspect of existence might not distinguish between the divine and the demonic. Culture plays a significant role in shaping these views. Christians who desire to participate in the miraculous should begin by examining their worldview and identifying any barriers.

The Influence of Worldview

People do not live in a culturally neutral society, neither do they encounter God in a vacuum. The world of the twentieth century is far from the Garden of Eden. Yet in this less than ideal world, believers are invited to encounter God and experience His power and kingdom. Their worldview influences their approach to this experience.

Missionary anthropologist Paul Hiebert defines "culture" as "the integrated system of learned patterns of behavior, ideas, and products characteristic of a society."[2] These patterns give rise to observable cultural expressions of people groups. Charles Kraft, another missionary anthropologist, defines "worldview" as "the culturally structured assumptions, values, and commitments underlying a people's perception of REALITY."[3] It is like the unseen foundation of a building or the base of an iceberg. Although not observable, a worldview is the system of accepted truths, or assumptions, that shapes one's values, perceptions, and behaviors. It is the lens through which everything, including one's self, is viewed.

Cultural values and worldviews affect how people define and relate to the supernatural as well as how they interpret Scripture. Interestingly, the non-Western worldview is closer to those of the Bible than is the modern, secular worldview of Euro-Americans. Non-Western peoples are better prepared to understand the tribal ties and rituals of the Old Testament cultures, and they place more emphasis on the spirit world. All societies must deal with the material world, the human world, and the spirit world; however, different people groups tend to focus on one area more than on the others. Most non-Western cultures seek to appease spirits or alter their activity. Euro-Americans, however, center their attention on conquering and manipulating the material world, likely ignoring or denying the existence and influence of the supernatural.

Perception influences interpretations and responses. People interpret and respond to their world according to how they have been taught. Culture is transmitted through the teaching-learning process, whether formally, informally, or nonformally. Role models and indoctrination play a significant part in how individuals perceive their world long before they begin to make choices. The admonition "Train a child in the way he should go" (Proverbs 22:6) underlines the importance of this process. In a child's early years, home, church, school, and significant others form the inclinations of a lifetime.

Religion is integral to culture. While a worldview provides basic assumptions about reality, religion offers the content of this reality. The religious dimension influences and shapes the whole of a culture, which in turn gives it shape; the relationship between religion and culture creates cause and effect, each impacting the other. Old Testament prophets warned of the potentially negative impact of this interaction. Israel enacted measures to avoid the contaminating influence of pagan culture.

Paul Hiebert laments the failure in missions to differentiate between the gospel and human cultures.[4] One of the great weaknesses of modern Christian missions occurs with mistaking the process of westernization for Christianization. The call to accept Christ and to follow Him in righteousness demands far more than a mere sociological change. The elevation of peoples' living standards might be a noble and worthy effort, but it does not change their relationship to sin. Christian faith constitutes more than a label or the adoption of a culture with its attendant worldviews. It involves a supernatural change of heart and a relationship to Christ, which lead to changes in behavior and worldview.

Acceptable and unacceptable behavior varies from culture to culture. Christians must critique their culture through the lens of the kingdom of God. Indeed, what constitutes sin and morality must be determined by biblical standards and not the mores of a society. Moral compromise of biblical principles renders the Church impotent. Samson, born to be a judge and deliverer, learned through experience how compromise brings shame, destroys vision, and makes one a slave (Judges 16:18–21). The believer who desires to minister in signs and wonders must recognize the stark contrast between the principles of the kingdom of God and those of this world.

Kraft points out the importance of distinguishing between culture and people. Although culture has no power of its own, its defined patterns do influence how people perceive reality. Individuals follow the script of their culture, empowered by the force of habit.[5] Because patterns of culture, including worldview, are learned, it is possible to change one's mind-set. Desiring the Israelites to become spiritual change agents in their cultural setting, God commanded them: "Consecrate yourselves and be holy, because I am holy" (Leviticus 11:44). While unpopular today, these instructions remain valid and pertinent. God reveals himself in might and power when Christians declare as Joshua did, "'As for me and my household, we will serve the Lord'" (Joshua 24:15). Furthermore, Jesus' prayer for His disciples clearly indicates that we are not called to withdraw from society: "'[Father,] my prayer is not that you take them out of the world but that you protect them from the evil one. They are not of the world, even as I am not of it. Sanctify them by the truth; your word is truth'" (John 17:15–17). The Church should be salt and light in the midst of society. This witness, however, will inevitably lead to a clash (power encounter) between the Kingdom of light and the kingdom of darkness.

Although people groups hold a common worldview—a significant body of shared assumptions—latitude exists for diversity within a group. These assumptions provide building blocks for constituting a given worldview and enable people to deal with basic areas of life. Sociologists and cultural anthropologists define these as "worldview universals." Kraft[6] identifies five of them and Hiebert[7] six. An understanding of these universals will benefit the believer in preparing for ministry in signs and wonders.

1. *Worldview provides a pattern for categorizing and classifying things and beings.* How people groups perceive reality varies. Euro-Americans, for example, usually classify objects as either animate or inanimate. However, the animist and a significant percentage of non-Westerners believe that everything, including rocks and trees, has life. Hindus believe insects have souls that are essentially the same as human souls. The distinction between what is natural and what is supernatural reflects the bedrock of one's worldview. When people classify the concept of a spirit world as mythological, they reject the reality of angels and demons and doubt the possibility of God's miraculous interventions.

2. *Worldview provides the focus for perceiving time and events.*

People groups differ about the quality of an event or the quantity of time spent. Time may be viewed as either linear, pendular, cyclical, or spiral. Euro-Americans define time as the linear progression of uniform increments, thinking in terms of being early, on time, or late for an event. Other cultures, including those of the biblical lands, think in terms of the event itself. Old and New Testament cultures were event-oriented; in these settings, corporate worship was event-experiences of the powerful presence of God.

3. *Worldview provides a pattern for relating to space and the material world.* This dimension impacts decisions relating to the use of space and the placement of material things, which may even have religious significance. God told Moses, "'Take off your sandals, for the place where you are standing is holy ground'" (Exodus 3:5). The Israelites considered the temple and its furnishings to be holy. Because mosques and Buddhist temples are considered holy, one is not allowed to wear shoes inside. In many areas of the world, such as Africa, Southeast Asia, and some of the Pacific islands, the location of a proposed building is determined by a spiritual leader who divines the wishes of the spirits.

Many Christians, among them John Wimber and other proponents of the Third Wave,[8] contend that demons have dominion over certain geographical regions that must be broken to allow effective ministry. C. Peter Wagner gives further insight: "Demons can and do attach themselves to objects, to houses and other buildings, to animals, and to people. Jesus found a legion of demons in one man and sent them into a herd of swine. Paul warned the Corinthians not to eat meat offered to idols in the idol temples, because they would risk fellowship with demons" (1 Corinthians 10:20).[9]

4. *Worldview provides a pattern for relating to individual versus group identity.* Euro-Americans often seek to establish individual identity apart from the family, clan, or group. To much of the world, the well-being of the extended family, the tribe, or even the nation are much more important than the individual's well-being. When presenting the plan of salvation, the Western approach expects each individual to decide to follow Christ; however, this idea is incomprehensible in cultures that think in terms of family decisions. As the "mission field" immigrates to the Western world, this idea significantly challenges the Church.

5. *Worldview provides a pattern for addressing causality.* This pattern of underlying assumptions explains forces at work in the universe and serves as a foundation for analyzing natural and supernatural causes. Issues that must be addressed relate to the natural world, the human domain, and the supernatural domain. These issues reflect the vast difference between scientific theories about the origin of the universe and life forms and biblical teachings on the activity of the Creator God. The materialistic and naturalistic views encountered in Western societies remain antithetical to the biblical presentation of the existence of non-material beings. The person who doubts the existence and activity of the supernatural will not automatically come to a new understanding upon praying the sinner's prayer of repentance. On the other hand, many non-Western societies place heavy emphasis on the domain of the supernatural and its viability, but that is not to say that supernatural activity in these societies is necessarily good or promotes righteousness. Indeed, it is often demonic, hostile to God and His kingdom!

6. *Worldview provides a pattern for establishing values.* Values govern the relative worth of ideas, ideals, or objects and can be of a moral, social, or religious nature. What is valued and to what degree varies from culture to culture. Euro-Americans, for example, prefer to value material possessions whereas many other cultures put greater value on intangibles, especially relationships. This mind-set affects an individual's relationship with God, by whether his or her priority is placed on the relationship or material blessings. What does one value most, the principles of God's kingdom or the views of a secular, humanistic society?

Our purpose is not to argue about any view's superiority, but to note that the believer's worldview influences preparation for and expectation of God's miraculous activity. One can prepare for signs and wonders, but it must be done intentionally. Diversity in congregations means differing worldviews, differences that must be considered in any discussion of supernatural powers.

Proper Motives

What motivates the believer's desire for the occurrence of signs and wonders? Is it merely an interest in the spectacular? Do some believers desire signs and wonders only to punctuate their ministry gifts to simply draw attention to themselves? In a world that is jaded with the spectacular, this must not be the case in the Church!

Two legitimate reasons exist for seeking signs and wonders. First, the believer desires that the name of the Sovereign Lord, and He alone, receive the praise and glory. God graciously intervenes in response to a believer's prayer as His gift to the person. Believers do not need a sign to validate the gospel because they already participate in its power: God gives signs and wonders to the nonbeliever, gifts to the believer. Neither the elder in Tabligbo nor we needed signs and wonders. However, because he desired healing, we empathized with him and prayed for that miracle.

Second, signs and wonders demonstrate God's power and lead nonbelievers to faith in Jesus Christ. The greatest of all signs and wonders happens when people are set free from the enslavement of sin and brought into a relationship with Jesus Christ, who announced at the synagogue in Nazareth, "'The Spirit of the Lord is on me, because he has anointed me to preach good news to the poor. He has sent me to proclaim freedom for the prisoners . . . to release the oppressed'" (Luke 4:18). In Tabligbo, we prayed for a miracle so that a village of nonbelievers could see the gospel. With proper motives we can request and expect signs and wonders.

Principles for Preparation

Preparation for signs and wonders becomes a journey of spiritual growth that leads to service. Individuals and church bodies can participate in the supernatural activity of God. Because this engages us in spiritual warfare (the kingdom of God versus the kingdom of Satan), principles rather than procedures guide our preparation.

1. *Practice righteousness.* In 2 Chronicles 7:14, God appeared to Solomon at the dedication of the temple and specified that if the people, who were called by His name, would "'humble themselves and pray and seek [His] face and turn from their wicked ways,'" He would hear them, forgive them, and heal their land. The writer to the Hebrews reminds believers that "without holiness no one will see the Lord" (Hebrews 12:14), neither should they

expect to see His power when they consistently ignore His call to holiness.

2. *Give yourself to prayer and fasting.* E. M. Bounds aptly says, "In the fearful contest in this world between God and the devil, between good and evil, and between heaven and hell, prayer is the mighty force for overcoming Satan, giving dominion over sin, and defeating hell."[10]

Jesus admonishes His followers to "ask and it will be given to you" (Matthew 7:7). More signs and wonders will occur when congregations and pastors ask boldly. Believers who truly believe that God will intervene in human circumstances should petition with clarity and confidence. It should be the kind of prayer that does more than recite self-gratifying requests, but intercedes on behalf of others. Linking fasting with prayer further emphasizes the believer's priorities.

3. *Become people of the Word so as to become people of faith.* Paul teaches that "faith comes from hearing the message, and the message is heard through the word of Christ" (Romans 10:17). The Word empowers! Believers who saturate themselves with the Word and its testimonies to "the mighty saving acts of God" will cry out for Him to do it again. And He will! Evidence abounds that what God has done He still does. Churches become places of power when people steeped in His Word come together.

4. *Emphasize worship as an event rather than a timed exercise.* True worship is an encounter with God in time that marks lives for eternity. When believers approach Him in private devotion and corporate worship, God consciousness must replace time consciousness. Time pales in importance to an encounter with the divine. Accounts of prayer and worship that continued for hours—even days—punctuate the history of revivals. Reordered priorities give full expression to the worship event, as happened at Southeastern College in 1970 during a morning chapel service as Joseph Wannenmacher (with his violin) and Birdie Kovacs (at the organ) played "The Holy City." As the music filled the auditorium, a hush settled over the congregation. Aware of the awesome presence of God, no one moved from the chapel for several hours. Students began to fall to their knees, weeping and crying out to God; powerful waves of His holy presence washed away scars of sin and healed the future of hundreds of students. Many testified of God's intervention in their lives. Classes and sched-

ules were interrupted for three days as God's event continued. What if the college administration and faculty had gone by the clock?

On the island of Patmos, John glimpsed the worship of the triumphant Church: "The twenty-four elders and the four living creatures fell down and worshipped God, who was seated on the throne. And they cried: 'Amen! Hallelujah!' Then a voice came from the throne, saying: 'Praise our God, all you his servants, you who fear him, both small and great!'" (Revelation 19:4–5). In the words of one famous preacher, "The church militant on earth must capture for itself the essential notes of the worship of the church triumphant."[11]

5. *Practice and promote "koinonia."* The Greek word *koinonia* means "fellowship" and conveys the sharing of a common bond, or relationship.[12] The biblical text portrays this bonding as the normative relationship between individuals who are themselves bonded to Christ. Luke presents a clear description of the fellowship among believers in the Early Church by emphasizing that they "had everything in common," and "many wonders and miraculous signs were done by the apostles." The fact that they "broke bread in their homes and ate together with glad and sincere hearts" serves as a fitting prelude to "the Lord [adding] to their number daily those who were being saved" (Acts 2:42–47).

It takes practice for the Church to become proficient at loving people and using things in a society that practices the inverse. However, *koinonia* means "family in action." The relationship between believers points to and relies on the relationship with Christ. Therefore, Christian fellowship promotes evangelism, which brings signs and wonders.

6. *Emphasize spiritual values.* What do believers value most? Jesus taught His followers to value and seek "His Kingdom" (Luke 12:31) and to be convinced that spiritual matters count more than material possessions. "For where your treasure is, there your heart will be also" (Matthew 6:21). Spiritual maturity does not come by chance but must be developed. The effort expended in spiritual development will determine the occurrence of the miraculous.

7. *Trust in God's power.* Doctrinal statements of most church bodies affirm God's omnipotence, His all-powerfulness. For signs and wonders to become normative, this must be more than men-

tal assent and represent the believer's faith and experience. No situation, problem, or disease exists beyond the possibility of God's power to change. The Psalmist said, "'How awesome are your deeds! So great is your power that your enemies cringe before you'" (Psalm 66:3).

8. *Recognize God's sovereignty.* God provides no intellectual escape hatch nor an apology when miracles fail to occur. He has not called the Church to defend His honor. Neither does He owe an explanation of why a petition is unanswered. Humans have limited perspective, but God sees all factors and does all things well. God can be trusted. He does not betray His nature or His people.

9. *Get involved in evangelism.* To catch fish, a fisherman must go to a lake and throw out a line and baited hook. Likewise, an obvious vantage point for witnessing signs and wonders comes from involvement in evangelism, bringing people from the power of Satan to God. Jesus told the Pharisees and teachers of the Law that their generation would have no miraculous sign other than "'the sign of the prophet Jonah'" (Matthew 12:39). Yet Jesus admonished His followers to "'go into all the world and preach the good news to all creation'" and included in His commission His promise that "'these signs will accompany those who believe: In my name they will drive out demons; they will speak in new tongues; they will pick up snakes with their hands; and when they drink deadly poison, it will not hurt them at all; they will place their hands on sick people, and they will get well'" (Mark 16:15–17). Mark summarizes the results of their obedience: "Then the disciples went out and preached everywhere, and the Lord worked with them and confirmed his word by the signs that accompanied it" (16:20).[13]

God works through the ordinary, the unseen, and sometimes the spectacular of signs and wonders. He employs a variety of gracious means to transform a life racked by pain and turmoil into one of health and peace, His gift to those who dare to believe and ask. God has been performing signs and wonders for centuries, yet each one occurs as new, fresh, and original. His miraculous interventions reveal to the human heart His nature and His activity. A life ready for the miraculous moves in a flow of communion with God that takes the believer beyond the realm of the natural into the realm of the supernatural.

Endnotes

[1]For documented accounts of contemporary signs and wonders, see Ralph W. Harris, *Acts Today: Signs & Wonders of the Holy Spirit* (Springfield, Mo.: Gospel Publishing House, 1995).

[2]Paul G. Hiebert, *Cultural Anthropology,* 2d ed. (Grand Rapids: Baker Book House, 1988), 25.

[3]Charles H. Kraft, *Christianity With Power: Your Worldview and Your Experience of the Supernatural* (Ann Arbor, Mich.: Vine Books, 1989), 20.

[4]Paul G. Hiebert, *Anthropological Insights for Missionaries* (Grand Rapids: Baker Book House, 1985), 53.

[5]Kraft, *Christianity With Power,* 56.

[6]Ibid., 203–205.

[7]Hiebert, *Cultural Anthropology,* 278.

[8]The first wave is identified as the classical Pentecostals, the second wave is the charismatics, the third wave is the mainline evangelicals who are embracing and experiencing the power of the Holy Spirit in life, worship, and Christian service. See C. Peter Wagner, *Third Wave of the Holy Spirit* (Ann Arbor, Mich.: Vine Books, 1988).

[9]C. Peter Wagner, "Territorial Spirits and World Missions," *Evangelical Missions Quarterly* 25 (July 1989): 278–288.

[10]E. M. Bounds, *The Possibilities of Prayer* (Grand Rapids: Baker Book House, 1979), 123. This book is one in a series of classic books on prayer written by Bounds.

[11]James S. Stewart, "The Relevance of Worship to Life" in *Classic Sermons on Worship,* comp. Warren W. Wiersbe (Grand Rapids: Kregal Publications, 1988), 73–83.

[12]Gerhard Kittel, ed. *Theological Dictionary of the New Testament,* vol. 3. (Grand Rapids: William B. Eerdmans Publishing Company, 1966), 789–809.

[13]Although textual questions have been raised about Mark 16:9–20, it is generally agreed that this passage is consistent with the corpus of the Gospels.

6

Faith for Effective Ministry

James D. Hernando

There exists no more essential concept to a biblical understanding of the Christian life than faith. It stands as the first requirement in our approach to God: "Without *faith* it is impossible to please Him, for he that cometh to God must *believe* that He is, and that He is a rewarder of those who diligently seek Him" (Hebrews 11:6). It is the main characteristic of those who live right before God: " 'The righteous will live by his faith' " (Habakkuk 2:4). Faith lies at the heart of God's call to salvation: " '*Believe* on the Lord Jesus Christ, and thou shalt be saved' " (Acts 16:31, KJV). It describes the means by which we receive salvation—"Whosoever *believeth* in him should not perish, but have everlasting life" (John 3:16, KJV)—and by which we enter into divine sonship with God—"But as many as received Him, to them He gave the right to become children of God, even to those who *believe* in His name" (John 1:12). Finally, Paul twice argues from the example of Abraham that God declares a person righteous based on faith in Christ (cf. Romans 3:19–4:25; Galatians 3:1–11).

Given the importance of faith to our Christian experience, the question, What role does faith play in signs and wonders? inevitably arises. Matthew raises it for us: "Coming to his [i.e., Jesus'] hometown He began teaching them. . . . And He did not do many miracles there because of their unbelief" (Matthew 13:54–58). Matthew draws a causal connection between Jesus' inability to do many miracles and the unbelief of the people of Nazareth.

To what extent, then, does faith determine whether the Church experiences signs and wonders? Those who answer this question lean toward one of two very different views of God's character and how He operates in response to faith. On one side stand those who emphasize the sovereignty of God and the rarity of miracles. Although God's power to work miracles is not in question, this side denies that He chooses to exercise that power today. They say that New Testament miracles occurred to validate the claims of the apostles concerning Christ, ceasing shortly after the apostolic period.[1]

On the other end of the theological spectrum stand those who see faith as determining whether or not the Church experiences miracles. They believe that the entire universe (physical and spiritual) is governed by certain immutable laws: Miracles belong to the supernatural, spiritual realm governed by the law of faith. Sinner and saint alike are subject to this law and can use it to achieve supernatural results.

Faith teacher Kenneth Hagin explains: "It used to bother me when I'd see unsaved people getting results. Then it dawned on me what the sinners were doing: they were cooperating with the law of God—the law of faith."[2] Elsewhere he writes, "In the final analysis, you see, it is my faith which determines the extent of my blessing."[3]

Hagin maintains such an exalted view of faith because he sees the Church as exercising the same universal power and authority that Christ possessed while on earth (Matthew 28:18) and which, after His ascension, He transferred to the Church. The Church now exercises this authority by speaking words of faith (Scripture) "in Jesus' Name."[4] Consequently, only the believer's faith limits what God can do.

Earl Paulk goes further in asserting that God is "bound" by the believer's faith. He sharply criticizes those who insist that God is not bound by law. "I strongly disagree with that premise . . . God limits Himself to work within the laws He ordains. . . . Man's obedience and faith toward God allow miracles—supernatural occurrences overriding natural laws—to occur."[5]

In view of seemingly opposite perspectives, this chapter seeks a truly biblical view of faith that avoids these polarities.

Faith in the New Testament

The first and basic scriptural definition of faith is "to believe and be convinced of" or "to trust someone or something." In both the Old and New Testaments the predominant meaning is religious: faith being directed toward deity—God and Christ. A better description of the usage might be relational, since faith in God or Christ presupposes a redemptive relationship between God and His people or Christ and His disciples. It is this sense that we see most clearly behind the New Testament's use of *pistis* ("faith") and *pisteuein* ("to believe") for describing what theologians call "saving faith." It is not merely mental assent to the facts about God's redemptive work in Christ, but involves a personal trust in Jesus to save us. For example, Nicodemus came to Jesus after having been confronted by His teachings and miraculous deeds. Nicodemus correctly assessed the facts and concluded that Jesus was a "teacher come from God" (John 3:2, KJV) but had yet to trust Him for salvation.

Second, because the New Testament emphasizes the object of the believer's faith, it is not surprising that *pistis* came to designate Christian faith (or Christianity itself; Acts 6:7) and, more narrowly, that body of doctrine which Christians believe (Galatians 1:23). This can be called the "content of faith," in that *pistis* defines what Christians believe, live, and teach.

A third use in Scripture relates to the character of faith. Here *pistis* generally denotes "faithfulness," the quality that allows someone to place complete confidence in another as trustworthy, dependable, and faithful.[6] It is applied to God (Romans 3:3), Jesus Christ (Romans 3:22),[7] and the believer (Titus 2:10). *Pistis* as "faithfulness" also appears among the "fruit of the Spirit" (Galatians 5:22).

A fourth use of *pistis* receives little attention within non-Pentecostal and noncharismatic circles. This is the "gift *(charisma)* of faith" uniquely presented by Paul in 1 Corinthians. It is given (12:4,7,9) and effected (v. 11) by the Spirit. Unlike relational faith, it is not practiced by every Christian but by select individuals in the body of Christ (vv. 11,20–30). In this context, *pistis* involves an unquestioning belief that God will come to our aid and deliver us with His miracle-working power. It is the kind of faith that can "move mountains" (13:2, NIV). Paul likely had in mind Jesus' words "'Truly I say to you, if you have faith as a mustard seed, you shall say to this mountain, "Move from here to there," and it shall move; and nothing shall be impossible to you'" (Matthew 17:20).

This fourth category of faith is a suitable launching pad for our discussion of faith and its relation to signs, wonders, and miracles. Paul's words suggest that such miracle-working faith is the sovereign work of the Holy Spirit. Jesus' words suggest that the burden rests on the believer's exercise of faith. It appears we have come full circle to the question we began with: Does faith have a determining role to play in whether the Church experiences signs and wonders?

Biblical Principles of Faith

Our study of the biblical words for faith points to several conclusions about the nature of true biblical faith, principles that prepare us to address the perplexing question above.

RELATIONSHIP WITH GOD

In Old and New Testament alike, God calls His people to live by faith. What constitutes a proper response of faith does not remain static throughout the Bible, but grows as God's revelation of grace and truth enlarges and the plan of redemption unfolds. Ultimately, this culminates in the advent and teachings of His Son (Hebrews 1:1–2). One common element in every faith response is trust and dependence upon God; biblical believers place their confidence in God.

In the Old Testament, a relationship of trust existed between God and His people. Yahweh summoned His people to a personal covenant with Him, because He is "the faithful God" and "keeps His covenant," and His loving-kindness *(hesed)* is unending (Deuteronomy 7:9; cf. 32:4). What God says and does reflects His nature and, therefore, is altogether trustworthy. This explains why God and His testimony (whether given in word, deed, or by prophetic messenger) are sometimes used interchangeably. Faith in God rests on the acceptance of divine testimony. To reject God's word or witness is to reject God himself. In Exodus 4, Moses complains to God that the people " 'will not believe me' " (v. 1). God assures him that signs would be granted

" 'that they might believe the Lord' " (v. 5). After God demonstrated these signs, we read, "It shall come about that if they will not believe you or heed the witness of the first sign, they may believe the witness of the last sign" (v. 8). Note that in the first half of the verse it is Moses that is to be believed and in the second half it is the witness of the sign. After the word of the Lord had been delivered to the people and the signs performed among them, the text states simply, "So the people believed" (v. 31).

The New Testament continues this unity and continuity between God, His word, His work, and His messenger. Jesus is the definitive and consummate Word from God (Hebrew 1:1–2).[8] His earthly ministry was filled with signs that attested to the fact that God was with Him (John 3:2; cf. Acts 2:22). No wonder John leaves us this sober admonition: "If we receive the witness of men, the witness of God is greater; for the witness of God is this, that He has borne witness concerning His Son. The one who believes in the Son of God has the witness in himself; the one who does not believe God has made Him a liar, because he has not believed in the witness that God has borne concerning His Son" (1 John 5:9–10).

Application to Signs and Wonders

Faith should never be viewed apart from its relational nature. When we believe God for signs and wonders in the Church, we must do so as redeemed children of God. It is His will we seek to do, His kingdom we seek to advance, His glory we seek to manifest. This was the posture of the first disciples when they prayed for signs and wonders: " 'Lord, take note of their threats, and grant that Thy bond-servants may speak Thy word with all confidence, while Thou dost extend Thy hand to heal, and *signs and wonders* take place through the name of Thy holy servant Jesus' " (Acts 4:29–30). The motive behind their petition was obedience to the will of God in bringing the gospel to all the world (Acts 1:8). They petitioned the Lord for boldness to speak His word.

Prayer is a relational activity and obedience is a relational response to the lordship of Christ. Our desire to see signs and wonders cannot avoid this dimension of faith, perhaps explaining why the disciples asked Jesus to "increase" their faith (Luke 17:5). His response (v. 6) about the awesome potential of even mustard-seed faith suggests that His disciples had in mind the special kind of faith that believes God to move mountains (Matthew 17:20). At first glance the illustration of the uncommended servant (Luke 17:7–10) does not seem to fit the context. However, if we understand the relational nature of faith, it is very appropriate. In a nutshell, the story teaches that obedience is the expected and only proper response of a true servant. The story, far from being incongruous, answers the request of the disciples in a profound way. Faith (even the mountain-moving kind) grows well in the soil of obedience and submission to the known will of God.

Returning to the disciples' prayer in Acts 4, we note another key ingredient. They saw their own experience of persecution as an extension of their Lord's: "'For truly in this city there were gathered together against Thy holy servant Jesus, whom Thou didst anoint, both Herod and Pontius Pilate, along with the Gentiles and the peoples of Israel, to do whatever Thy hand and Thy purpose predestined to occur'" (vv. 27–28). The disciples did not deny their dire circumstances, giving an accurate account of their plight. What is remarkable is not so much their acceptance of reality as their acknowledgment that the current persecution was within the providence of God. Their petition for signs and wonders was made in full submission to the will of God, even if it included personal suffering.

Formulaic faith that virtually eliminates God as a relational player in the equation or reduces His role to one that is subservient to the believer and his faith is patently unscriptural because it denies one of the essential attributes that make Him God—His sovereign lordship.[9] While God may choose to act in response to the believer's prayer and faith, He is never presented in Scripture as being bound by it. Thus, faith seeks supernatural intervention in pursuit of God's will and in humble submission to His sovereignty.

RIGHT BELIEFS ABOUT GOD

The relational and subjective dimension of faith is sometimes set at odds with what some have called "objective faith," that is, when *pistis* designates statements of faith or truths that the first Christians believed, confessed, and taught. Actually, the two aspects of faith are complementary and inseparable. The writer to the Hebrews says that "without faith it is impossible to please Him, for he who comes to God must believe that He is, and that He is a rewarder of those who seek Him" (11:6). Coming to God and believing are the relational aspects of faith.

However, believing also has a propositional object of truth about the God who is approached in faith, specifically, His existence and the nature of His response. J. I. Packer sees these two aspects of faith as logically dependent. He asserts that "some belief about the object trusted is the logical and psychological presupposition of the act of trust itself, for trust in a thing reflects a positive expectation about its behavior, and rational expectation is impossible if the thing's capacities for behavior are wholly unknown."[10] So then, "saving faith" requires some knowledge concerning who Christ is and what He has done to provide salvation.

Paul echoes this truth in Romans 10:14: "How then shall they call upon Him in whom they have not believed? And how shall they *believe* in Him whom they have not *heard*?" Some acquaintance with the facts of Jesus' life, death, and resurrection is necessary for an adequate presentation of the gospel. And through its proclamation, God is pleased to save those who believe (1 Corinthians 1:21).

To be sure, merely knowing and giving mental assent to that message is insufficient. Christian faith requires a personal commitment of trust in the resurrected and living Christ. Nevertheless, the quality of our faith in God is in some measure dependent on what we believe about Him. What God has revealed in Scripture about himself and His redemption through Jesus Christ should not only inform our faith but enhance and deepen our relationship with Him as well.

Application to Signs and Wonders

In assessing the role faith plays in signs and wonders, the temptation is to let experience rule. Some feel that a theology of signs and wonders is adequate only when supported by mountains of anecdotal evidence. Proponents of the modern faith movement routinely begin with some sort of miraculous or revelatory experience and work their way forward to a theological assessment of that experience.[11] Sometimes this assessment is aided by new, but unorthodox, interpretations of Scripture.

An adequate theology of signs and wonders must rest upon the teachings of Scripture. When the biblical data is comprehensively examined, a remarkable paradox emerges. Faith can be both present and absent in the petition for signs and wonders. People are both commended (Acts 4:24–31) and censured (Matthew 12:39; 16:4) when petitioning the Lord for signs. Signs and wonders both encourage and strengthen faith (Acts 4:29–30; cf. John 10:37) and are met with doubt, unbelief, and rebellion (John 6:30; 12:37). They can represent the authentic work of God, witnessing to the presence of the Kingdom and the truth of the gospel (Matthew 12:28), or witness to a false gospel, false Christs, and the deceiving presence of the evil one (2 Thessalonians 2:9).

When we examine all relevant biblical texts, one crucial observation emerges: Whether signs and wonders appear in Scripture in a positive or negative light depends on the identity of the petitioners, the motive for their asking, and the focus of their faith. Jews, Pharisees, Sadducees, scribes, and Herod all asked Jesus for a sign, yet came without true biblical faith. They came demanding a sign before they would believe His claims (John 6:30). Some demanded a "sign from heaven" to test Him (Mark 8:11). Others made the request to challenge His authority (John 2:18) or to satisfy their idle curiosity (Luke 23:8). Even some of Jesus' would-be disciples asked, "'What then do you do for a sign, that we may see, and believe you? What work do you perform?'" (John 6:30). A common denominator among them was a refusal to believe unless it was on their own terms. The irony lies in the fact that prior to such demands, Jesus had been performing signs, wonders, and miraculous deeds. But these were not acceptable. They demanded a sign that met with their approval. Jesus rebuked them by calling them an "'evil and adulterous generation'" (Matthew 16:4) and refused to give them a sign (Mark 8:12). Why? The character of their faith was not genuine, neither was He the object of their faith.

Modern-day Christians seeking to promote the presence of signs and wonders in the Church need to ask a probing question: Are we believing in miracles of one kind or another, or in the God who reveals himself in and through the miraculous? Let us follow the example of the disciples in Acts 4. They turned to God in prayer, believing that He would manifest the authority and power of the resurrected Christ. Faith for signs and wonders must ultimately be faith in God. Faith looks to the Scriptures in order to discern the divine nature and redemptive purpose in all the manifestations of His power and presence.

RIGHT CONDUCT TOWARD GOD

Faithfulness in the Old Testament is a theological concept. The Septuagint uses *pistis* mainly to describe the faithfulness of God, but even when describing people, the context is always their conduct toward God.[12]

The New Testament uses *pistis* only once of God (Romans 3:3) and three times of people in their response toward God (Matthew 23:23; Galatians 5:22; Titus 2:10). More often faithfulness is conveyed by the adjective *pistos*. On numerous occasions it is applied directly to God,[13] to Christ,[14] or to sayings or words about Christ.[15] Most frequently *pistos* characterizes people in their "faithful" response to Christ or God.[16] The picture that emerges is clear. God is faithful. He has entered into a redemptive relationship with His people, those who believe in Christ and trust Him for salvation. In turn He expects them to be faithful.

Application to Signs and Wonders

We must still ask, How is faithfulness measured? The answer lies in doing the will of God. Paul declared his thankfulness to Jesus Christ for considering him faithful and putting him into the service of the gospel (1 Timothy 1:12). To the church in Corinth, he commends Timothy as a "faithful child in the Lord" who will remind them, says Paul, "of my ways which are in Christ, just as I teach everywhere in every church" (1 Corinthians 4:17). Paul's ministry in Corinth, while initially successful, soon found antagonists in the persons of self-declared teachers who challenged both his teachings and his claim to apostleship. In 2 Corinthians 10 through 13, Paul takes up a polemic against those he labels "false apostles, deceitful workers," and those "disguising themselves as apostles of Christ" (2 Corinthians 11:13). In defense of his own apostleship he writes, "The *signs of a true apostle* were performed among you with all perseverance, *by signs and wonders and miracles*" (2 Corinthians 12:12).

Many Pentecostals and charismatics assume that the "signs of a true apostle" in the first half of the verse are the miraculous signs, wonders, and miracles of the second half. Although the word for "signs" is the same in both places, there are good reasons to conclude Paul meant something different: (1) The word has a wider range of meanings than just "miracles."[17] (2) The grammar of this verse indicates that the terms at the end of the sentence describe the manner in which the signs of a true apostle were performed.

To what then do the first signs refer? In chapters 10 through 13 Paul has been pointing out the marks of true apostolic ministry. In addition to spiritual power to confront evil (10:3–4,8–11; 13:2–4,10), they include such traits as (1) jealous care for the churches (11:2), (2) true knowledge of Jesus and His gospel (11:6), (3) sacrificial self-support so as not to burden the churches (11:9), (4) absence of self-serving or heavy-handed discipline (11:20–21), (5) willingness to suffer and be afflicted for the cause of Christ (11:23–29), (6) divine (visionary) revelations (12:1–6), and (7) patient endurance of the "thorn in the flesh" (12:7–9).[18]

It should be noted that the "pseudo-apostles" (11:13) could and probably did make claims to revelations and superior knowledge of the truth (11:5–6; 12:1–7). They came disguised by Satan as "ministers of righteousness" (11:15, KJV). Perhaps they also came with counterfeit signs effected by Satan. Nevertheless, when defending his apostleship, Paul does not point to miracles, but to the Christlikeness of his personal character and ministry. These qualities marked Paul as a true apostle of Christ in contradistinction to all self-seeking pretenders to that office.[19]

The lesson for those desiring to see signs and wonders in the Church should be obvious: Supernatural manifestations are integral to, but not the definitive mark of, New Testament apostolic ministry. Signs and wonders must be judged as to their true source or origin. One key way of judging is to discern the character of the ministers (and their ministry) through whom these signs and wonders appear.

EXPECTATION OF GREAT THINGS FROM GOD

Earlier we encountered the special gift *(charisma)* of faith given sovereignly by the Holy Spirit to individual members of

Christ's body (1 Corinthians 12:9,7). It is the mountain-moving kind of faith that Paul (13:2) and Jesus speak of (Matthew 17:20; 21:21). This category of faith is unusual because of the magnitude of what Jesus says can be accomplished. He repeatedly affirms that the potential of such believing prayer is unlimited. If such faith is present, He says, " 'Nothing shall be impossible to you' " (Matthew 17:20; cf. 21:22). Regarding the impossibility of the rich being saved, Jesus states, " 'With men this is impossible, but with God all things are possible' " (Matthew 19:26). To the desperate father seeking deliverance for his demon-possessed son, Jesus says, " 'All things are possible to him who believes' " (Mark 9:23).

At this point we should recognize that there is a kind of faith that Jesus condemns and one that He glowingly commends. When Jesus' disciples failed to cast a demon from a man's son and privately asked Him why they could not do it, He answered, " 'Because of the *littleness of your faith*' " (Matthew 17:20). To fearful Peter sinking beneath the waves, Jesus said, " 'O you of *little faith*, why did you doubt?' " (Matthew 14:31). A doubting spirit seems to be connected with littleness of faith. To the bewildered disciples staring at the withered fig tree, Jesus said, " 'Truly I say to you, if you have faith, and *do not doubt*, you shall not only do what was done to the fig tree, but even if you say to this mountain, "Be taken up and cast into the sea," it shall happen' " (Matthew 21:21). In all these examples Jesus lamented and even castigated smallness of faith.

Elsewhere Jesus commended great faith. To the Roman centurion who refused Jesus' offer to go and heal his servant but said, " 'Just say the word, and my servant will be healed,' " Jesus exclaimed in amazement, " 'Not even in Israel have I found such *great faith*' " (Luke 7:7,9). One truth becomes evident: Jesus expects faith from His disciples. Chiding them for their little faith also served as encouragement to believe in Him and trust God to do the impossible. The reference to the faith of the disciples was not an assessment of quantity but of character. Their faith was little because it was wavering and unsure, influenced by doubt and the stark reality of seemingly hopeless situations. Similarly, the centurion's faith was not great because of quantity but because of quality, it was great in its character. He was totally convinced that Jesus could heal his servant and was prepared to take Him at His word.

Application to Signs and Wonders

What makes the difference between little and great faith? The answer begins with the recognition that the distinction lies in the character of one's faith. Mark's version of the faith-that-moves-a-mountain saying suggests part of the answer. It reads, " *'Have faith in God.* Truly I say to you, whoever says to this mountain, "Be taken up and cast into the sea," and does not doubt in his heart, but believes that what he says is going to happen, it shall be granted him' " (Mark 11:22–23). Both the context and the grammar of the sentence make it clear that Jesus is exhorting them to believe in God, that is, to set Him as the object of their trust and faith.

It is not, as some suggest, an exhortation to possess some mystical God-kind-of-faith that springs from His divine nature and is imparted to us.[20] Nor is it the kind of faith that God himself possesses and through which He created the world out of nothing.[21] Nowhere do the Scriptures teach that God shares this unique aspect of His role as Creator with humanity. Miracles, signs, and wonders are the prerogative of God alone. Miracles are never the work or creation of a human being. They are never at the sovereign disposition of a person, to be commanded, confessed, or claimed at will. Yet when believers who have received the outpouring of the Spirit from the exalted Lord (Acts 2:33) seek to fully preach the gospel in the power of the Spirit (Romans 15:19), they will turn to God in faith and expect great things from Him, even signs and wonders.

Endnotes

[1]This view is known as "cessationism," and the close of the apostolic period is usually marked by the writing of the last book of the New Testament canon. See John MacArthur Jr., *Charismatic Chaos* (Grand Rapids: Zondervan Publishing House, 1992), 60–61.

[2]Kenneth E. Hagin, *Having Faith in Your Faith* (Tulsa: Faith Library Publications, 1980), 3–4. Hagin's view of faith is more complex than what can be presented here. In actuality, it arises from his doctrines of Scripture, the Godhead, the Atonement, and humankind, and borrows

heavily from the works of E. W. Kenyon whose eclectic theology dipped into the cultic streams of such metaphysical cults as New Thought and Unity. See Daniel R. McConnell, *A Different Gospel: A Historical and Biblical Analysis of the Modern Faith Movement* (Peabody, Mass.: Hendrickson Publishers, 1988), 15–29; Dale H. Simmons, *Hagin— Heretic or Herald of God,* M.A. thesis, "A Theological and Historical Analysis of Kenneth E. Hagin's Claim to be a Prophet," for Oral Roberts University, 1985, 56–78.

[3]Kenneth E. Hagin, *What to Do When Faith Seems Weak and Victory Lost* (Tulsa: Faith Library Publications, 1979), 18.

[4]Kenneth E. Hagin, *Prevailing Prayer to Peace* (Tulsa: Faith Library Publications, 1973), 17.

[5]Earl Paulk, *That the World May Know* (Atlanta: K. Dimension Publishers, 1987), 101–102.

[6]J. P. Louw and E. A. Nida, eds., *Greek-English Lexicon of the New Testament: Based on Semantic Domains,* 2d ed. (New York: United Bible Societies, 1989), 2:377.

[7]There is considerable debate over whether the phrase *pistis Christou* should be rendered "faith in Christ" or "the faithfulness of Christ." While both translations are grammatically possible, the Septuagint usage of *pistis* strongly favors the latter. For a full discussion see Gabriel Herbert, "Faithfulness and Faith," *Theology* 58 (September 1955), 372–379; D. W. B. Robinson, "Faith of Jesus Christ—A New Testament Debate," *Reformed Theological Review* 29 (1970), 71–81.

[8]In the New Testament Jesus is much more than a prophet of God. In Jesus there is no clearer revelation of God (John 1:18), since "He is the radiance of God's glory and the exact representation of His nature" (Hebrews 1:3). "He is the image of the invisible God" (Colossians 1:15) in whom "all the fulness of Deity dwells in bodily form" (Colossians 2:9). He is a self-declared prophet of God (Matthew 13:57) whose words and deeds are in unity with the Father (John 5:20–30; cf. 8:28,42).

[9]The absolute sovereignty of God is amply attested to throughout the Scriptures, e.g., 1 Chronicles 29:1; Psalm 115:3; Isaiah 45:9; Matthew 20:15; Romans 9:14–21; 11:26; Ephesians 1:11; 1 Timothy 6:15–16; and Revelation 4:8–11.

[10]J. I. Packer, "Faith," in *Evangelical Dictionary of Theology,* ed. Walter A. Elwell (Grand Rapids: Baker Book House, 1984), 400.

[11]See McConnell, *Different Gospel,* 57–76, where he historically traces the alleged nine visitations of Jesus experienced by Kenneth Hagin and the subsequent developments in his theology. Cf., Simmons, *Hagin,* 29–54.

[12]This is the case even when the assessment is negative. Thus, Israel is judged as a "perverse generation, . . . in whom is no faithfulness *[pistis]*" (Deuteronomy 32:20).

[13]1 Corinthians 1:9; 10:13; 2 Corinthians 1:18; 1 Thessalonians 5:24; Hebrews 10:23; 11:11; 1 Peter 4:19; 1 John 1:9.

[14]Hebrews 2:17; 3:2; 3:6; Revelation 1:5; 3:14; 19:11.

[15]1 Timothy 1:15; 3:1; 4:9; Titus 1:9; 3:8; Revelation 21:5; 22:6.

[16]Eight times the adjective is used in a secular sense of a faithful servant (Matthew 24:45; 25:21,23; Luke 12:42; 16:10–12; 19:17), but even here they appear in parables that illustrate the fidelity a believer is to have in the kingdom of God. Twenty-one times it is used of people in their response to the Lord (Acts 16:15; 1 Corinthians 4:2,17; 7:25; Galatians 3:9; Ephesians 1:1; 6:21; Colossians 1:2,7; 4:7,9; 1 Timothy 1:12; 3:11; 2 Timothy 2:2,13; Hebrews 3:5; 1 Peter 1:21; 5:12; Revelation 2:10,13; 17:14).

[17]See Romans 4:11 on circumcision, 2 Thessalonians 3:17 on Paul's signature, and Matthew 26:48 on Judas's kiss.

[18]For a thorough exegetical treatment of this issue see Wayne Grudem, "Should Christians Expect Miracles Today," in *The Kingdom and the Power: Are Healing and the Spiritual Gifts Used by Jesus and the Early Church Meant for the Church Today?*, ed. Gary S. Greig and Kevin N. Springer (Ventura, Calif: Regal Books, 1993), 63–66.

[19]Ibid., 65.

[20]See E. W. Kenyon, *The Two Kinds of Faith: Faith's Secrets Revealed* (Lynwood, Wash.: Kenyon Publishing Society, 1969), 103. Given the biblical emphasis on the object of faith, one is at a loss to explain to whom or to what God directs His faith.

[21]K. E. Hagin, *New Thresholds of Faith* (Tulsa: Faith Library Publications, 1972), 74. For an excellent survey of the doctrine of faith in the modern faith movement see McConnell, *Different Gospel*, 134–147.

7
Naturally Supernatural
Benny C. Aker and Edgar R. Lee

An iceberg breaks off a glacier, the bulk of it undersea, stabilizing the visible portion as it rides the ocean's current. Signs and wonders are like an iceberg, being but the tip of other supernatural activity—regeneration, baptism in the Spirit, the gifts of the Spirit. For example, in John 3 Nicodemus, an eminent leader and teacher of the Jews, broke rank with his colleagues and secretly came to Jesus one evening, confessing his belief that Jesus was a teacher who had come from God. In contrast to his unbelieving friends in the Sanhedrin, he concluded that Jesus' "signs," John's word for "miracles," validated His commission and message since "no one could perform the miraculous signs [he was] doing if God were not with him" (John 3:2).

Rather than indulging Nicodemus's interest in miracles, which had now served their purpose in leading him to faith, Jesus turned his attention to an essential event, equally supernatural but never called a miracle, the new birth. So important is this quiet miracle that one cannot even see the kingdom of God without it.[1]

The Nicodemus story reminds the believer that faith is rooted firmly in the supernatural work of God. Some happenings are so obviously supernatural, so different and rare in the natural order of things, that we refer to them as "miracles" or "signs and wonders." But the quiet miracle of regeneration serves as the foundation of God's work in the world. Indeed, all of Christian life and ministry should be "naturally supernatural."

The Baptism of the Spirit

After the death of Jesus, the spread of Christianity in the Mediterranean world, from Jerusalem to Rome, during the first thirty years or so was nothing short of phenomenal. Few imagined that the scattered followers of the crucified Nazarene, none of whom were world-class leaders with wealth or political connections, could turn the world upside down (Acts 17:6, KJV). But the Book of Acts records that the supernatural wisdom and power of God's Spirit energized their efforts. In the daily routine of professional clergy in modern institutional settings, people often forget that ministry must still be done in the same way. Like the disciples, believers today need the "enduement" of power: the baptism in the Spirit (Acts 1:8).

The Book of Acts provides the historical narrative of the expansion of the Church, which occurred as a result of the mighty power of the Spirit, working signs and wonders through inspired witness and various gifts.[2] Luke, the author, suggests that Spirit baptism had become not only distinguishable from regeneration but also scarce, negatively impacting world evangelization.[3] Through several themes that Luke emphasizes, he gives hints as to why people had not received.

First, people were not praying for it (a practical problem).[4] So to counteract that, Luke emphasizes prayer. Second, some did not believe in Spirit baptism (a theological issue), a problem that surfaces in Acts 19 where John the Baptist's disciples say they had never heard of the Holy Spirit. Since they had earlier heard John say that Jesus would give them the Spirit, they either had not believed in or heard of Spirit baptism as Jesus had distinctly promised. Thus, they had become a Christian sect—believing in Jesus but not in His Spirit baptism.[5] Third, religious factors may have discouraged early Christians from seeking Spirit baptism. For example, magic played a large part in the ancient world with its powerful mystical and spiritual elements that many found attractive (see Acts 8:4–24 where Simon the magician wanted such controlling power).[6] To counteract this fear, Luke made sure that people linked legitimate spiritual activity with the true God and distinguished it from pagan phenomena. According to Acts 3, Peter and John performed signs and wonders through the laying on of hands in the name of Jesus. Luke argues in the narrative of his Gospel and Acts (especially in Acts 2) that spreading the gospel and delivering sinners requires the baptism in the Spirit.

At the beginning of Acts, Luke sets forth Spirit baptism as the pattern of the Spirit's coming on the Day of Pentecost. It does not refer to conversion initiation (salvation) as James Dunn suggested some time ago,[7] nor does it indicate the beginning of the Church, as understood by some Pentecostals and evangelicals.[8] Instead, Luke establishes a theology for empowered ministry through his narrative. Acts 2 demonstrates that with the coming of the Spirit there is a pattern for Christians to follow in their worldwide mission, with some of these elements explicitly or implicitly mentioned later in the book.[9] In particular, two things shape this pattern: (1) Spirit empowerment for signs and wonders and (2) inspired witness of the exalted Christ. The latter refers to speaking in tongues, which testifies that God has exalted Jesus to His right hand. He is now Lord over all with full authority. He is the Head of the Church with the right to pour out the Spirit on believers.[10] In turn, this empowers His disciples to preach the gospel and perform signs and wonders, highlighting that a major purpose of speaking in tongues centers on evangelization.

Awareness of the placement of Acts 2 in the book's narrative and an analysis of its structure reveals the emphasis. First, the chapter distinguishes itself through its time boundaries and begins by saying, "When the day of Pentecost had fully arrived. . . ."[11] Luke devotes the entire chapter to the Feast of Pentecost and the arrival of the Spirit.[12] This inaugural event projects a pattern for understanding Spirit-empowered apostolic activity. Acts differs from other narratives in that it contains no climax, deliberately leaving it open-ended, without closure.

Acts 2 contains its own special narrative structure, including (1) characters—Peter and the visiting people; (2) conflict—the coming of the Spirit causes a host of differing responses, especially confusion (2:5–13); and (3) a climax—the conflict finds resolution (2:37–41).

Peter's three-point sermon, beginning in verse 14, explains and removes the confusion of the observers. The first point (vv. 14–21) notes that the coming of the Spirit fulfilled an Old Testament promise about the day of salvation. Anyone can now call upon the

Lord to be saved. Point two (vv. 22–28) explains that the death and resurrection of Jesus brought salvation. Point three concludes that (vv. 29–36) since Jesus had ascended to the right hand of God and received all authority, He had poured out the Spirit to enable His disciples to evangelize the world (see Acts 1:8).[13] Tongues served as evidence that Jesus, who gave the Spirit to inspire the apostles to speak of the crucified, risen, and exalted Lord, had received this authority from God the Father. When Spirit-filled believers speak in tongues, they witness that Jesus rules as Savior.

Gifts of the Spirit

The theological development of Acts signals that the Spirit's outpouring brought a profusion of spiritual gifts for ministry. Acts 2 highlights an important moment in the history of the Church with a special sign of the Spirit's presence and activity: The disciples "began to speak in other tongues as the Spirit enabled them." The verb in 2:4, *apophthengomai,*[14] translated "enabled," denotes the prophetic speech that Moses referred to when he said: "'I wish that all the Lord's people were prophets and that the Lord would put his Spirit on them!'" (Numbers 11:29). Later, the word of the Lord came through the prophet Joel, saying, " 'I will pour out my Spirit on all people. Your sons and daughters will prophesy' " (2:28). Peter emphasized this relationship between prophecy and the Spirit in Acts 2:18 where he added, *"and they will prophesy"* (not found in the Hebrew text).

Having shown no such previous ability and manifesting the gift of prophecy in his address to the crowd at Pentecost (Acts 2:14–41), Peter announced the fulfillment of Joel's prophecy. His newfound ability points to the descent of the Spirit and the subsequent gift of prophecy. When stating that Peter "addressed the crowd," Luke again used the verb *apophthengomai* to denote prophetic inspiration (2:14), thereby emphasizing that the Spirit had now been given to persons of both genders, all ages (2:17–18), and all people groups who come to faith in Christ. William Larkin suggests that "prophecy for Luke encompasses Spirit-filled speaking in other languages (2:12,16), predictive discourse (11:27; 21:10–11; compare 9:10; 10:10; 16:9; 18:9, where dreams and visions guide the post-Pentecost church) and proclamatory witness (15:32)."[15] Similarly, Paul witnessed to inspired speech as a significant gifting in the New Testament community (1 Corinthians 14:1,5).

The Book of Acts records a diversity of powerful gifts flowing out of the Pentecost event. Amazement struck people as the apostles performed "many wonders and miraculous signs" (2:43; 5:12–16). But the Spirit empowered others besides the Twelve: Stephen did "great wonders and miraculous signs" (6:8). Philip brought revival to Samaria through "miraculous signs" (8:6) and "great signs and miracles" (8:13), which included exorcisms and the healing of many paralytics and cripples (8:7). Ananias prayed for the healing of Saul (9:17–18). Paul exercised a ministry of miracles as evidenced in the blinding of the Jewish sorcerer Bar-Jesus (13:6–11), the healing of the crippled man at Lystra (14:8–10), the exorcism of a spirit at Philippi (16:16–18), the "extraordinary miracles" of Ephesus (19:11–12), the raising of Eutychus at Troas (20:9–10), and the healing of the sick of Malta (28:8–9).

Miracles of deliverance also took place in the releases of Peter (12:5–19) and Paul (16:26) from prison. Peter became supernaturally aware of the deception of Ananias and Sapphira (5:3). The Spirit enabled Peter (4:8ff.) and Stephen (6:10) to be powerful speakers and apologists. Remarkable guidance came at strategic junctures, as in the sending of Paul on his missionary task (13:1–3), the receiving of directions along the way (16:6–10), and the receiving of timely visions that encouraged and directed him (18:9–10; 28:23). Members of his congregations were prompted by the Spirit to tell Paul of his impending imprisonment (20:23; 21:4,10–11). When divisive problems like the issue over benevolence (6:1–6) and Gentile circumcision (15) threatened to rend the young Church, great wisdom and skill effected satisfactory resolutions. Prophets other than the Twelve, like Agabus (11:28; 21:10), Barnabas, Simeon, Lucius of Antioch (13:1), Judas, and Silas (15:32), also came forward. Philip had four daughters who prophesied (though not explicitly called prophets [21:9]).

This "narrative theology" of spiritual gifting in Acts is also verified by the "didactic theology" of the New Testament letters. In Ephesians, for example, Paul demonstrates that the risen and ascended Christ distributes spiritual gifts of leadership to equip God's people for ministry (Ephesians 4:7–13; cf. 1 Corinthians

15:3–8), including ordinary laypersons. The Spirit gives them to facilitate spreading the gospel of Christ. As E. Earle Ellis aptly points out, "The gifts of the Spirit are the function of the Spirit that Paul identifies with Christian ministry. They enable believers to fulfill the *mission* of Christ."[16]

These gifts are most commonly identified in the New Testament by the Greek term *charisma,* denoting "spiritual gift" in no less than twelve of its seventeen occurrences.[17] Hence we often refer to the gifts as the *charismata.* Occasionally, the Greek words *pneumatikon* (1 Corinthians 12:1; 14:1) and *doma* (Ephesians 4:7) refer to "spiritual gift." The New Testament contains several "gift lists" (Romans 12:6ff.; 1 Corinthians 12:8ff.; 12:28ff; Ephesians 4:11; cf. 1 Peter 4:10–11 where gifts appear to be categorized as "speaking" and "serving"). Herman Ridderbos offers valuable insights into the importance of *charisma* in Paul's theology of ministry: "*Charisma* is everything that the Spirit wishes to use and presses into service for equipping and upbuilding the church, what can serve for instruction and admonition and for ministering to one another, or even the effective direction and government of the church. The whole distinction between charismatic and non-charismatic ministries in the church therefore cannot be reconciled with the Pauline conception of *charisma.*"[18]

The gifts then are widely distributed to all of God's people, not just to clergy: Paul says that "to each one the manifestation of the Spirit is given for the common good" (1 Corinthians 12:7). And Peter says, "Each one should use whatever gift *[charisma]* he has received to serve *[diakoneo]* others, faithfully administering God's grace *[charis]* in its various forms" (1 Peter 4:10).

The nine gifts of the Spirit, often mistakenly thought to be the only spiritual gifts, are enumerated in 1 Corinthians 12:8ff.: the word of wisdom, the word of knowledge, faith, gifts of healing(s), the working of miracles, prophecy, the discerning of spirits, different kinds of tongues, and the interpretation of tongues. Several of these gifts appear in all three lists: Romans 12, 1 Corinthians 12, and Ephesians 4. Paul presents them as supernatural and spontaneous. They are both a "manifestation" of the Spirit and "are given" (passive voice) by the Spirit (1 Corinthians 12:7–8). Although requiring faith, these gifts are uniquely supernatural.

Though they are not as well known, Paul identifies other equally important spiritual gifts: serving, teaching, exhortation, giving, ruling, showing mercy (Romans 12:7–8), helping, and governing (1 Corinthians 12:28). Paul also apparently considered his chastity a gift from God, which enabled him to minister more effectively (1 Corinthians 7:7). These gifts also have their origin in the work of the Holy Spirit and provide essential equipment for the ministry of the Church. Unlike the more obviously supernatural "nine gifts," they reside in believers and should be used regularly, energetically, and conscientiously without dependence on a spontaneous quickening of the Spirit. They provide tools for the "nuts and bolts" work of the Church.

Although most of the needs of the Church may be met through these gifts, the lists are not comprehensive. For example, the Old Testament notes that the Holy Spirit invested gifts of craftsmanship in Bezalel and Oholiab for furnishing the tabernacle (Exodus 31:1–11). The creative Spirit of God, facing an everchanging world, can surely grant additional gifts more or less unique to every new situation if needed. Certainly the New Testament goes to great pains to show a variety of gifts: "There are different kinds of gifts . . . different kinds of service *(diakonia)* . . . different kinds of working *(energema)*" (1 Corinthians 12:4–6).

The secrets of success for the Early Church can be found in the Spirit's gifts working through committed believers. Although certain apostolic endowments were probably unique to the founding of the Church and the establishment of the canon of Scripture, the Spirit poured a profusion of *charismata* upon leaders and laity, male and female, equipping them for continuing dynamic ministry.

Until recently, many evangelicals have insisted that miracles ceased with the last of the apostles and that spiritual gifts have been muted.[19] In fact, no sound biblical rationale exists for the cessation of the Spirit's power and gifting in the modern Church;[20] the Spirit's gifts continue as the tools for effective ministry. A merely professional ministry, no matter how accomplished, is inadequate for the task, and for that reason the ministry of the Church must always be a supernatural one. Although men and women must prepare to the best of their ability, they should lend themselves eagerly and naturally to the work of the Spirit of Christ through gifts, sometimes miraculous but always present—and powerfully effective.

Endnotes

[1]"See" in John 3:3 means the same as "enter" in v. 5. The parallel construction of these verses makes this evident.

[2]See also Hebrews 2:4.

[3]Jesus, anointed for his ministry in Luke 3:21–22, models the believer's ministry in Acts 2.

[4]Luke's gospel mentions prayer more than Matthew's and Mark's and records Jesus praying long periods of time before announcing important decisions. In Acts, when Christians pray, the Lord comes in mighty power.

[5]See Ben Aker, "New Directions in Lucan Theology: Reflections on Luke 3:21–22 and Some Implications," *Faces of Renewal,* ed. Paul Elbert (Peabody, Mass.: Hendrickson Publishers, 1988), 108–27.

[6]This condition shows up in Africa, for instance, where the church is growing rapidly but often pastors fear going too far into the spirit world.

[7]James D. G. Dunn, *Baptism in the Holy Spirit* (London: SCM Press, 1970). Howard M. Ervin later responded in *Conversion-Initiation and the Baptism in the Holy Spirit* (Peabody, Mass.: Hendrickson Publishers, 1984).

[8]The non-Pentecostal holiness evangelicals who hold to a second work of grace take Acts 2 to refer to sanctification and a kind of empowerment; John 20:19–23 speaks of salvation, the first work. See the *Wesleyan Bible Commentary,* Matthew-Mark-Luke-John-Acts (reprint, Peabody, Mass.: Hendrickson Publishers, 1986), 4:468, 504–505. Many Pentecostals from this tradition take the coming of the Spirit and the tongues of fire in Acts 2 to refer to the initiation of the Church and a special Pentecostal empowerment as well as a sanctifying experience. Richard N. Longenecker in "Acts," ed., Frank E. Gaebelein, *The Expositor's Bible Commentary* (Grand Rapids: Zondervan Publishing House, 1981), 268–69, takes a mediating position, noting that it is not quite accurate to refer to this one event as the birthday of the Church. He notes that power for ministry also occurs in this text. Pentecostals, though, commonly see in Acts 2 the birth of the Church. Howard M. Ervin, *Spirit Baptism: A Biblical Investigation* (Peabody, Mass: Hendrickson Publishers, 1987), chapter 7 and pages 68–69, sets forth a good biblical position in which the disciples were born again by Jesus' breathing on them some days earlier. In Acts 2, they were empowered for service. Many others also support this view; see, for example, George T. Montague, *Holy Spirit* (Peabody, Mass.: Hendrickson Publishers,

1976), chapter 22; and Stanley M. Horton, *What the Bible Says About the Holy Spirit* (Springfield, Mo.: Gospel Publishing House, 1976), chapter 7. For example, Ernest S. Williams, *Systematic Theology* (Springfield, Mo.: Gospel Publishing House, 1953), 3:100, says that the Church began on Pentecost. This belief probably originated from dispensationalism, not from the holiness tradition.

[9]The tongues of fire and the sound of wind are not among the elements of this pattern. In the narrative they serve to emphasize the "programmatic," dramatic arrival of the Spirit in the Messianic Age. I prefer this term to "precedent"—in fact I choose not to use this term because it doesn't fit the evidence in Luke-Acts. "Paradigmatic" is even more useful. In the first edition of *How to Read the Bible for All It's Worth* (Grand Rapids: Zondervan Publishing House, 1982), by Gordon D. Fee and Douglas Stuart, Fee uses the term "precedent" in the title of chapter 6; also in his *Gospel and Spirit: Issues in New Testament Hermeneutics* (Peabody, Mass.: Hendrickson Publishers, 1991), 83–104.

In the second edition of *How to Read the Bible* (1993), Fee has not changed his position but makes the following changes: The chapter title has changed from "Acts: The Problem of Historical Precedent" to "Acts: The Question of Historical Precedent"; in the first paragraph of p. 96, he added one sentence to include Luke's use of narrative; Fee rewrote the second paragraph and lengthened it a bit to include something on Luke's theological interests. The second paragraph on p. 96 has been slightly reworded and enlarged. And on p. 110, the second paragraph has been enhanced considerably; on the same page under #3 he adds a statement that allows for the repetition of some patterns to speak in a normal but not normative manner for the contemporary church. Thus, Fee has spoken clearly on authorial intent, something that he emphasized in *Gospel and Spirit*. This goes along with his view on the genre issue. See William Klein, Craig L. Blomberg, and Robert L. Hubbard, Jr., *Introduction to Biblical Hermeneutics* (Dallas: Word Publishing, 1993), 344–45; and the excellent material in chapter 32 of *A Complete Literary Guide to the Bible,* ed. Leland Ryken and Tremper Longman III (Grand Rapids: Zondervan Publishing House, 1993). The former reject Fee and Stuart's view of Acts, 349–50.

[10]Another purpose is the Pentecostal doctrine of initial, physical evidence.

[11]Author's translation. In translations, the clause in the two places does not appear identically; nonetheless, in Greek it is the same adverb of time. Except for this reference, this construction occurs only in Luke 9:51 ("As the time approached . . .").

[12]Chapter 3 covers another time. This feast occurs at no other place in Acts.

[13]He received the Spirit. It is thus not correct, contra some scholars, to see in this account a confusion with Luke 2:21–22.

[14]Gerhard Kittel, ed., *Theological Dictionary of the New Testament,* I, trans. and ed. Geoffrey W. Bromiley (Grand Rapids: William B. Eerdmans Publishing Company, 1964), 447.

[15]William J. Larkin, *Acts,* Inter Varsity Press New Testament Commentary (Downers Grove, Ill.: InterVarsity Press, 1995), 54.

[16]E. Earle Ellis, *Pauline Theology: Ministry and Society* (Grand Rapids: William B. Eerdmans Publishing Company, 1989), 34.

[17]See Romans 1:11; 12:6; 1 Corinthians 1:7; 7:7; 12:4,9,28,30–31; 1 Timothy 4:14; 2 Timothy 1:6; 1 Peter 4:10; cf. Romans 11:29.

[18]Herman Ridderbos, *Paul: An Outline of His Theology,* trans. John Richard De Witt (Grand Rapids: William B. Eerdmans Publishing Company, 1975), 442. See also Siegfried Schatzmann, *A Pauline Theology of Charismata* (Peabody, Mass.: Hendrickson Publishers, 1987).

[19]For a recent statement of this view, see Edmund P. Clowney, *The Church* (Downers Grove, Ill.: InterVarsity Press, 1995), 237–268.

[20]For recent critiques of the cessationist position, see Jack Deere, *Surprised by the Power of the Spirit* (Grand Rapids: Zondervan Publishing House, 1993), 229–252; and Wayne Grudem, *Systematic Theology: An Introduction to Biblical Doctrine* (Grand Rapids: Zondervan Publishing House, 1994), 1031–1046.

8

Spiritual Warfare

Edgar R. Lee

A late-night phone call that turns into an encounter with a snarling demon will rapidly shake one's complacency about the spirit world. That happened to me a number of years ago after a routine day as a suburban pastor. Just before retiring for the night, and while my wife was still being debriefed by our daughter who was just home from a date, the bedside telephone rang and a young woman with a soft, sweet voice began to ask for pastoral guidance. As we talked, her voice suddenly changed and became chillingly guttural, obviously demonic, and very threatening. My blood ran cold and, with my stunned wife and daughter looking on, my face turned white from shock.

With the help of the Holy Spirit, I quickly realized what was happening and, rebuking the demon who kept breaking into the conversation, arranged for the girl to come to our church for what I anticipated would be a brief deliverance session. With precious little experience but with earnest prayer and study, we soon plunged into the most bizarre encounter of our lives—and certainly one of the most instructive. The young woman's condition proved to be very similar to that of the Gerasene demoniac (Mark 5:1–20), with many different demonic personalities of varying powers and identities manifesting themselves through her. My encounter with her, and a couple of other demonized persons about the same time, opened a new dimension of signs and wonders for me. It also shook my limited knowledge of demonology to the core and forced a new study of Scripture and the literature.

The Unseen Enemy

The Bible clearly teaches the existence of an unseen enemy devoted to the destruction of humanity. He is most commonly referred to by the name "Satan," meaning "accuser," and as the "devil," meaning much the same: "adversary" or "slanderer." Other designations abound: "tempter" (Matthew 4:3), "evil one" (Matthew 5:37; Ephesians 6:16), "god of this age" (2 Corinthians 4:4), "serpent" (2 Corinthians 11:3), "ruler of the kingdom of the air" (Ephesians 2:2), and "enemy" (1 Timothy 5:14). People in Jesus' time called him Beelzebub, "prince of demons" (Matthew 12:24,27), and Paul referred to him once as Belial (2 Corinthians 6:15).

In the Old Testament, we assume Satan actively opposed God and His people, though his presence is rarely revealed. God, at the end of His creative activity, pronounced His creation "very good" (Genesis 1:31), which may mean that Satan, usually understood to have been a high-ranking angel originally created good, had not yet fallen. In any event, early in Genesis we find "the serpent," understood by the New Testament writers to be Satan (see 2 Corinthians 11:3 and Revelation 12:9ff.; 20:2), working to deceive Adam and Eve (Genesis 3:1ff.). Much later, this evil personality appears by his name, Satan (literally "a satan"), and incites David in a moment of arrogance to number Israel, resulting in a plague killing seventy thousand men (1 Chronicles 21:1; cf. 2 Samuel 24:1).

When Job struggled to make sense of the tragedies that overtook him, the inspired writer allowed the reader to see what Job could not: the real villain behind all his misfortune was the invisible Satan, who reveled in his role as accuser and adversary (Job 1:6ff.). However, the writer of the book clearly understood that the Lord limited the activities of Satan—undoubtedly to accomplish His own purposes of growth in Job's life. The adversary, while intelligent, is not omniscient, knowing everything as God does, nor is he omnipresent, being everywhere as God is, nor is he omnipotent, having all power as God does. In fact, in the Book of Job we discover that God keeps this powerful but finite being on a tight leash—a profound theological insight!

Satan's final Old Testament appearance occurs in one of Zechariah's visions (3:1–10). The high priest, Joshua, who represents the people of God, stands before the angel of the Lord in filthy garments. Predictably, Satan also stands there as the behind-the-scenes accuser—and not without grounds for doing so since the filthy garments attest to Joshua's human sinfulness. Only the justifying election of God results in Joshua's being clothed with clean, rich garments and being admitted to the courts of the Lord.

Demons, like Satan, seldom receive mention in the Old Testament; nevertheless, they lurk behind the idol worship of the times. Striking out against Israel's sin, Moses charged, "They . . . angered him with their detestable idols" and "sacrificed to *demons*" (Deuteronomy 32:16–17). Looking back on that time, the Psalmist adds, "They sacrificed their sons and their daughters to *demons*" (Psalm 106:37). Paul similarly understood that idolatrous sacrifices were offered to demons (1 Corinthians 10:20). No formal linkage appears in the older testament between the devil and demons, but in the light of the New Testament, we observe them to be allied in opposition to God and His people.

The activities of the devil and demons gain more attention in the New Testament. The devil appears early on as the tempter of Jesus only to be decisively defeated at the outset by our Lord's single-minded commitment to the Word of God (Matthew 4:1ff.; Luke 4:1ff.). Shortly after, the Gospels record that casting out demons became a very important part of Jesus' ministry (Matthew 4:24; Mark 1:21ff.; Luke 4:31ff.). In fact, He understood His exorcisms, done in the power of the Holy Spirit, to be definitive signs of the presence of God's kingdom (Matthew 12:28).

Peter's strategic sermon in the house of Cornelius presents the ministry of Jesus as a frontal attack on satanic oppression. After our Lord was "anointed . . . with the Holy Spirit and power," He not only "went around doing good," but He also healed "all who were under the power of the devil" (Acts 10:38). John makes a similar point: "The reason the Son of God appeared was to destroy the devil's work" (1 John 3:8). The writer to the Hebrews connects Satan's defeat to the Incarnation and the cross: "He [Jesus] too shared in their humanity [i.e., that of God's children] so that by his death he might destroy him who holds the power of death—that is, the devil—and free those who all their lives were held in slavery by their fear of death" (Hebrews 2:14–15).

Though decisively defeated at the cross and destined for eternal punishment in the lake of fire (Revelation 20:10), the devil remains throughout the Church Age the invisible but dangerous and implacable foe of believers. "Your enemy [*antidikos,* "adversary at law," "enemy"] the devil prowls [*peripateo,* "walks"] around like a roaring lion looking for someone to devour [*katapino,* "swallow," "swallow up," "devour," "overwhelm"]" (1 Peter 5:8). Believers should carefully note the calculated violence in this metaphor of the devil's conduct.

While the devil may be likened to a hungry lion stalking crippled prey, he rarely appears that way to his intended victims. He is usually incognito, always camouflaged and deceptive, and not infrequently very attractive to the weak and gullible. Warning the Corinthians against slick-talking false apostles "masquerading as apostles of Christ," Paul notes that "Satan . . . masquerades as an angel of light" (2 Corinthians 11:14). In other words, he usually tempts us with that which seems very normal, attractive, and appealing to both our reason and our senses.

A huge demonic force also attacks believers. Paul learned, "Our struggle is not against flesh and blood, but against the rulers *[archai],* against the authorities *[exousiai],* against the powers *[kosmokratores]* of this dark world and against the spiritual forces *[pneumatika]* of evil in the heavenly realms" (Ephesians 6:12). Paul also identifies certain "angels" *(angeloi)* and "powers" *(dunameis)* among these evil forces (Romans 8:38). Increasingly, scholars link his references to "rulers of this age" *(archontes,* 1 Corinthians 2:6,8), "thrones" *(thronoi,* Colossians 1:16), and "powers" *(kyriotetes,* Colossians 1:16; Ephesians 1:21) to evil powers. D. G. Reid observes, "The names themselves suggest some possibility that they refer to echelons of power within the spiritual world, but if that is the case, the evidence is insufficient to determine their ranking."[1]

The existence of an organized satanic kingdom, probably hierarchical, may also be inferred not only from Paul's references above but from other biblical data.[2] People referred to the devil as "Beelzebub, the *prince* of demons" (Matthew 9:34; 12:24; Mark 3:22; Luke 11:15), which Jesus seemed to legitimize by referring to Satan's kingdom (Matthew 12:26; Luke 11:18). In the Gospel of John, the devil is frequently called the *"prince* of this world" (12:31; 14:30; 16:11). Luke connects the expulsion of demons to

Satan's defeat, apparently showing his rulership of them (10:17ff.). To Paul, Satan is the *"god* of this age" (2 Corinthians 4:4) and the *"prince"* (KJV) or *"ruler* of the kingdom of the air" (Ephesians 2:2). John in Revelation presents Satan as a dragon with a huge army of angels determined to lead "the whole world astray" (12:7–9).

It has become fashionable to refer to certain members of this hierarchy as "territorial spirits."[3] C. Peter Wagner understands the Ephesian goddess, Artemis, also called Diana, to be such a territorial spirit. Paul accordingly engaged in strategic-level spiritual warfare against her (Acts 19:23–41).[4] While Scripture does not teach directly the necessity of identifying these spirits by name and waging deliberate spiritual warfare against them, there is some evidence for the existence of powerful geopolitical angelic powers. Among the evil spiritual powers in Ephesians 6:12 are "the powers of this dark world," the *kosmokratores,* more literally "world rulers." Such a description seems particularly apt for the powerful, evil angels in view when Daniel's messenger conflicts with the "the prince of Persia" and "the prince of Greece" (Daniel 10:13,20). By contrast, Daniel discovers a protector for Israel in the angel Michael, known as "one of the chief princes" (10:13), "your prince" (10:21), and "the great prince who protects your people" (12:1). Both G. B. Caird and F. F. Bruce consider the Greek translation of Deuteronomy 32:8 to represent the original:[5] "He set *the bounds of the peoples* according to *the number of the angels of God.*" Bruce comments, "This reading implies that the administration of the various nations has been parcelled out among a corresponding number of angelic powers."[6]

Victorious Spiritual Warfare

As they face this dark kingdom, those whose hearts are set on Christ have already enlisted the powerful aid of Him who "appeared . . . to destroy the devil's work" (1 John 3:8) and already experience the promise that "the one who is in you is greater than the one who is in the world" (1 John 4:4). Christians need not be preoccupied with such devil trivia as learning all the demons' names and ranks or practicing repeated exorcisms to rid themselves and others of evil tendencies. They will find no biblical admonitions to map and target every territorial demon with offensive prayer. If specific prayer and ministry strategies are needed in satanic strongholds at home or abroad, the Spirit surely will come to the aid of sensitive believers with biblically viable solutions.

The Bible presents a simple, though demanding, pattern for victory over the enemy. In Paul's language, the Christian takes up impenetrable armor, which God has already provided. That armor consists of "the belt of *truth*," "the breastplate of *righteousness*," the footwear of "the *gospel* of peace," "the shield of *faith*," "the helmet of *salvation*," "the sword of *the Spirit*, which is *the word of God*," and regular prayer *"in the Spirit"* (Ephesians 6:13–18). This equipment is nothing other than devout and disciplined Christian living in the power and wisdom of the Spirit and the Word. In contrast to the militancy of much spiritual-warfare language used today, the armor is primarily defensive. Rather than "search and destroy," Christian soldiers take a "stand against the devil's schemes" and "stand [their] ground" (6:11,13).

As in any battle, Christians must be alert to the nature and strategies of the adversary. If we are "unaware of his schemes" (*noema*, "method," "design," "plot"), as Paul notes, then Satan might indeed "outwit [*pleonekteo*, "take advantage of," "cheat," "get the better of"] us" (2 Corinthians 2:11). In fact, the apostle strongly commands us to "stand against the devil's schemes [*methodeia*, "trickery"]" (Ephesians 6:11), which may be particularly acute in "the day of evil" (6:13).

Subject to temptation, believers face a clever adversary who exploits human weaknesses for his own destructive purposes. Common but sinful actions, like nursing anger, "give the devil a foothold" (Ephesians 4:27). He knows how to steal the Word of God from our hearts (Matthew 13:19; Luke 8:12). The devil even takes advantage of our good-hearted mistakes. Peter, for example, could not bear to think of Jesus' predicted sufferings and unwittingly became a stumbling block (Matthew 16:23).

Scripture unfolds a threefold temptation model captured in a commonly used phrase: "the world, the flesh, and the devil." People live in a social environment, "the world," which exists in deliberate ignorance of, if not open hostility toward, God (1 John 2:15–16) and encourages them in similar thought and behavior. They also live in physical bodies, "the flesh," with legitimate natural desires which, if unchecked, can find sinful expression. In addition, "the devil" tempts people by direct appeal. Obviously he has to carry on the work of temptation through demons since he is not omnipresent and cannot simultaneously harass five billion people.

Citing James's assertion that "each one is tempted . . . by his own evil desire" (1:14), some assume that the devil has little or nothing to do with temptations that flow from the world and the flesh. But taken as a whole, the Bible shows that Satan not only introduced sin into the world, he and his fallen minions participate in all temptation. John declares flatly, "He who does what is sinful is of the devil, because the devil has been sinning from the beginning" (1 John 3:8). James taught that evil attitudes such as "bitter envy and selfish ambition" come from "the devil" (James 3:14). According to Paul, the "ruler of the kingdom of the air," the devil, is the "spirit who is now at work in those who are disobedient" (Ephesians 2:2). Those who oppose biblical truth taught by humble and conscientious Christian leaders fall into a "trap of the devil" (2 Timothy 2:26) and face the risk of following "deceiving spirits and things taught by demons" (1 Timothy 4:1). "The source of evil tendencies is both internal and external to people as well as supernatural," states Clinton E. Arnold, adding, "The demonic explanation for evil behavior needs to be seen as the thread that ties together all the evil influences."[7]

One does not have to look very far in Scripture to find examples of those who were spiritually shipwrecked by allowing the devil to tempt them through very ordinary means. Spiritually naive and unaware of his impending denial, which Jesus predicted, Peter did not comprehend the meaning of the saying, "Simon, Simon, Satan has asked to sift you as wheat" (Luke 22:31). Judas, the treasurer of the Twelve, became greedy for money, stole from the common purse, and, just before the betrayal of Jesus, "Satan entered Judas" (Luke 22:3; John 13:3). When Ananias and Sapphira lied about their giving, Peter told Ananias that Satan had filled his heart (Acts 5:3). The two immediately met an untimely death.

Though few Christians realize it, the devil plays a role in the discipline of unrepentant believers who fall into flagrant sin. In response to a notorious case of incest in the Corinthian church, Paul commanded the congregation to "hand this man over to

Satan, so that the sinful nature may be destroyed and his spirit saved on the day of the Lord" (1 Corinthians 5:5). The backslider had fallen into the trap of scandalous sexual temptation; now the one who tantalized him would be his tormentor. Hopefully, he would learn the devastation of unrestrained passion and repent of his sin.

The Enemy Revealed

While the devil usually operates unseen and unrecognized, he occasionally comes out of the closet in overt activity. Jesus, not uncommonly, encountered demon-possessed persons in the synagogue who recognized Him and became agitated by His presence, fearful of their final judgment (Mark 1:23ff.; cf. Luke 4:33ff.). A slave girl with a spirit of divination met Paul and his colleagues at Phillipi and introduced them as "servants of the Most High God" (Acts 16:16–17). From time to time, modern believers may encounter demon-possessed persons without warning and in unexpected places. My first encounter occurred in the living room of a parishioner's home, where I had been invited to witness to a neighborhood friend, whom I discovered to be under the influence of alcohol.

We read and hear far more reports of demons in other lands. While not easily documented with reliable statistics, however, overt demonic activity seems more apparent than ever in the United States. Several factors contribute to this development: (1) A general moral decline readily observable in the media's fixation on sex and violence. (2) Alcoholism and drug addiction, both of which lower moral inhibitions and contribute to personal and social depravity. Significantly, drug use appears to be connected in Scripture with the occult. The word *pharmakeia,* which denotes "enchantment with drugs,"[8] is found among the New Testament "vice lists" and translated by the NIV as "witchcraft" (Galatians 5:20), "magic arts" (Revelation 9:21) and "magic spell" (Revelation 18:23). Likewise, *pharmakoi* is rendered "enchanters with drugs" and "those who practice magic arts" (Revelation 21:8; 22:15). In my limited experience with demonized persons, drug and alcohol abuse are common. (3) "New age" religion with its emphasis on occult activities, such as channeling and seeking the help of "spirit guides,"[9] which many consider to be demon possession. The popular Doonesbury comic strip graphically represents this practice. One of its featured characters occasionally reverts to a previous "reincarnation," experiences a dramatic personality change, and rages hatefully at some unlucky person. (4) The influx of immigrants from third-world countries whose native religions foster belief in various spirits.

When Christians encounter real demon possession, they usually have little doubt about it. They may detect it in two ways: (1) by observing the activities and conversation of the one possessed and (2) by the spiritual gift of distinguishing between spirits (1 Corinthians 12:10). The first has to do with objective phenomena, which may be observed and described, the second with the inner voice of the Spirit. And while one or the other way of knowing may predominate in a given situation, the two will often function together because the Holy Spirit in the believer has a mysterious way of sensing and communicating the presence of evil as (or before) observation of demonic behavior takes place.

As I talked about Christ to the alcoholic mentioned earlier, she responded repetitiously in a very normal voice by saying, "I don't understand that concept." She could not or would not think about Jesus. Suddenly, like a bolt from the blue, came certain knowledge, undoubtedly the Spirit's gift of discernment, that this woman had a demon. This was a totally new experience, but I immediately stood and in Jesus' name commanded the demon to depart. The woman shrieked and fell to the floor. Other than her calm refusal to acknowledge "that concept," no other symptoms of possession appeared.

Well-documented and easily recognized phenomena, described in Scripture and repeated in deliverance literature, usually accompany demon possession. Demons, like those in the Geresene, characteristically react verbally and physically to the name and presence of Jesus (Mark 5:7). Other well-attested phenomena include supernatural strength, as in the Geresene's breaking of his chains (5:4); various personalities and voices, illustrated by the demons begging Jesus to send them into the pigs (5:12); self-destructive impulses, exhibited when the Geresene cut himself with stones (5:5); bizarre behavior, like living among tombs (5:3); and supernatural information, which in the Geresene is seen in his preknowledge of Jesus (5:7). While not omniscient, demons are very intelligent and apparently have the ability to observe and exchange information.

Scripture also occasionally attributes certain medical conditions to demonic affliction. For example, Matthew 17:14–18 records the story of an epileptic boy who suffered from seizures that caused him to fall into fire or water (characteristic of demonic, self-destructive impulses). Jesus also ministered to a crippled woman whose real problem was that she was "crippled by a spirit" (Luke 13:11) and "bound" by Satan (13:16), even while she was described by Jesus as "a daughter of Abraham." Not all, or even most, physical afflictions are demonic in origin, however, for the Gospel writers normally make a careful distinction between sickness and demonic affliction (Matthew 4:24; 8:16; Mark 1:32; Luke 4:40–41).

We should always remember that any one, or even a combination, of the common symptoms above does not necessarily indicate demonic activity. Some mental illnesses may exhibit symptoms similar to demon possession,[10] so careful observation and sensitivity to the guidance of the Holy Spirit should precede any deliverance. Consultation with experienced Christian ministers and psychologists in difficult and uncertain cases will also be helpful. Responsible believers will not traumatize a person by incorrectly describing him or her as demon possessed.

The Miracle of Deliverance

When directly confronted by evil spirits, believers may be secure in knowing that Christ has commissioned them to rout the spirits. Jesus gave the Twelve and the larger group of seventy-two "power and authority to drive out all demons" (Luke 9:1). When they returned with enthusiastic testimonies, saying, "Lord, even the demons submit to us in your name," Jesus provided both affirmation and caution. "I have given you authority to trample on snakes and scorpions and to overcome all the power of the enemy. . . . However, do not rejoice that the spirits submit to you, but rejoice that your names are written in heaven" (Luke 10:17–20). The closing verses of the Gospel of Mark continue to reflect the belief of the Early Church that driving out demons accompanies the preaching of the gospel as a sign of God's redemptive power (Mark 16:17).

Exorcisms continue in Acts as a normal function of apostolic ministry (Acts 5:16). When Philip began his ministry in Samaria, miraculous signs were prominent: "With shrieks, evil spirits came out of many" (Acts 8:7). Paul exorcised a spirit of divination from the Philippian slave girl (Acts 16:16–18), with such ministry also noted in Ephesus (Acts 19:12). Among the spiritual gifts mentioned by Paul is "miraculous powers" (1 Corinthians 12:10). Exorcism is often grouped among these miracles and doubtless employs other spiritual gifts as well.

The Acts narrative also includes the debacle of those who would plunge into this difficult area without proper grounding in personal faith. Seven sons of a Jewish chief priest named Sceva, like other Jewish exorcists in Ephesus, tried to follow Paul's example of commanding evil spirits to leave, using "the name of Jesus, whom Paul preaches." The text does not say how much prior success these apparently unconverted men enjoyed, but on one occasion they encountered a particularly violent spirit who challenged them with, "Jesus I know, and I know about Paul, but who are you?" (Acts 19:15). Rather than bowing to these unbelievers and their attempted exploitation of Jesus' name, the spirit endowed his host with supernatural strength and gave each of the presumptuous exorcists a severe beating. Exorcism is indeed done in the name of Jesus but only by believers acting in the power of His Spirit.

These guidelines will be helpful:

1. Only mature and knowledgeable Christian ministers or laypersons should engage in deliverance ministries.
2. Prayer, fasting, and studying the Scriptures are prerequisites to spiritual sensitivity and power.
3. Good advance planning will offset potentially disruptive side effects. Some mature helpers may be needed to gently but firmly restrain sufferers and prevent them from harming themselves. Others can assist with prayer and spiritual counsel—and also serve as witnesses. The location should be where phenomena such as loud shrieks, profanity and blasphemy, and bizarre and sometimes violent behavior are minimally disruptive. Avoid difficult exorcisms in public worship services if possible.
4. Preparation of the person seeking deliverance is crucial.

While there may be occasions when we are moved to sudden action, like Paul's deliverance of the Philippian slave girl (Acts 16:18), it usually pays to ascertain that the demonized person wants to be free, will turn to Jesus, and will renounce any sin connected with demonic activity. In fact, such an individual may be able personally to cast the demon out and should be invited to do so. The more the victim collaborates, the more certain the result.

While no one method of exorcism will fit every situation, the following charge is basic:

1. *"In the name of Jesus Christ . . ."*
2. *"I command you . . ."* Confidently and decisively claim the authority given by Christ, remembering that powerful demons frequently resist, argue, threaten, bluster, and initially refuse to depart. Quietly but firmly and repeatedly, without attempting to match the demon in sound and fury, *command* the demon(s) to leave.
3. *"the spirit of _____"* In difficult cases, it may be helpful or even necessary to ascertain the identity of the demon(s). My own experience, as well as my study of the literature, has shown that demons often verbally identify themselves with a particular attitude, action, or object. In the incident related at the beginning of this chapter, my colleagues and I encountered one demon who called himself Molech, the Ammonite god of child sacrifice (Leviticus 18:21; 1 Kings 11:7). Another claimed association with divination, still another with tarot cards. Others identified themselves with specific attitudes, like rejection.

    Recently, I preached in a church where a young woman in the service had recently been through deliverance and radiantly shared what Christ had done for her. The pastor and his wife told me her story over lunch. Obviously distraught, she had come to a Wednesday night service, and when the pastor's wife approached her for prayer, the battle was on! Surprised and inexperienced, this first lady of the parsonage nonetheless found a tremendous sense of the Spirit's presence and successfully commanded a series of demons to depart. Before leaving, however, the defiant spirits demanded that she first identify them and, to her amazement, in each case the Holy Spirit gave her their names.

4. *"to depart!"* I, like many others, have experienced some demons bargaining for their destination, much as the demons in the Geresene bargained with Jesus before entering the pigs (Mark 5:7–13). In the absence of firm biblical guidelines, we should be sensitive to the Holy Spirit in our responses. Since multiple possessions often occur, make certain that all spirits have departed.

Strange events commonly accompany exorcisms, particularly when powerful spirits are involved. The victim may pass out or vomit. In most instances, a piercing shriek signals the spirit's departure. The literature also abounds with reports of strange noises, unpleasant odors, moving objects, and so forth.

After the deliverance, insure that the individual repents, accepts Jesus Christ as Lord, and receives the Holy Spirit. Warn them about the way spirits seek to repossess their victims with a sevenfold vengeance (Matthew 12:43–45). Stress the importance of immediately breaking habitual behavioral problems of the past and beginning a discipline of Scripture reading and prayer. The fellowship and training of the church are essential to complete deliverance.

Christians and Demonization

A controversial issue in our day has been the question of whether or not Christians can be demon possessed. Merrill F. Unger's *Biblical Demonology,* published in 1952, maintained that while demons may possess unbelievers, Christians may be attacked only "from without, through pressure, suggestion, and temptation."[11] By 1971, however, Unger's research led him to revise his earlier opinion and conclude that believers could not only be oppressed but "actually suffer infestation by evil spirits."[12] That opinion echoed among many in the charismatic movement. Thus, a popular book by Frank and Ida Mae Hammond also stated, "Christians can be and are indwelt by demons."[13] Casting demons out of Christians quickly became popular—and controversial; exorcism seemed to offer a quick fix for all personal and moral problems.

Recent studies by a number of key leaders have led to a more carefully nuanced position, like that of Timothy M. Warner: "My study and experience have convinced me that a Christian may be attacked by demons and may be affected mentally and sometimes physically at significant levels, but that *this does not constitute possession or ownership.*"[14]

Warner, Unger, and Kenneth Hagin,[15] among others, all attempt to bring a more biblical perspective to the widespread reports of various demonic phenomena among people professing faith in Christ. They point out correctly that the New Testament does not have a word that means literally "demon possessed." Rather, it uses "to be demonized *[daimonizesthai],*" or "to have a[n evil/unclean] spirit/demon." Our modern understanding of literal possession by a demon accurately describes what happened to certain demonized persons (e.g., the Geresene [Mark 5:1ff.]); but "possession" is not intrinsic to the words themselves even though many lexicons offer that meaning.[16] The biblical context must determine the meaning of the word and the extent of demonization. Therefore, to have some demonic affliction is not necessarily to be demon possessed.

Some limit the apparent "demonization" of Christians by utilizing a trichotomous understanding of human nature: body, soul, and spirit (as in 1 Thessalonians 5:23). They argue that demons may invade the body and/or the soul but *never the spirit,* which, in the case of a believer, God by His Spirit indwells (e.g., Hagin, Unger, and Warner).[17] However, since the Bible does not clearly differentiate between the terms "spirit" and "soul" and frequently uses them interchangeably, trichotomy has never been the prevailing view of the Church. Most evangelicals think of a human being as a dichotomy, body and soul/spirit.[18] In any event, no Scriptural evidence warrants the assumption that an evil spirit can invade the soul but not the spirit.

It is probably better to explain demonic attacks against human beings on a continuum, as shown below, ranging from the less to the more severe.

Less Severe ———————————————————— More Severe

(1) Temptation (2) Oppression (3) Obsession (4) Possession

Along this continuum, several categories may be used to more specifically indicate various levels of demonic involvement and, perhaps, bring greater clarity to the discussion. Of the various categories found in the literature,[19] I prefer the following: (1) *Temptation*. Demonic forces as well as carnal desires tempt all persons. (2) *Oppression*. Demons probably intensely attack all persons from time to time in all kinds of circumstances, from economic problems to family tragedy to personal illness, as they did Job and Paul (2 Corinthians 12:7). (3) *Obsession*. Demons, in this case, may exert an obsessive influence over the thought and actions of persons guilty of recurring sinful actions or attitudes. New converts coming out of occult or degraded backgrounds may not immediately be delivered from obsessive demonic conditions that sometimes border on possession. (4) *Possession*. In this extreme condition, one or more demons actually indwell a person and from time to time seize direct control of thought, speech, and action.

Demonic Influence on Human Life

I believe that the devil and his legions regularly tempt and occasionally oppress Christians. But believers with a vital personal relationship with Christ are *never possessed*. In some circumstances, however, new converts from occult or degraded backgrounds may not immediately be freed of all demonically obsessive behaviors and may need deliverance.[20] This phenomenon is widely reported overseas with converts from folk religions. Moreover, nominal Christians or believers who fall into sinful patterns of behavior from which they willfully refuse to repent may also find themselves open to demonic obsession.[21] One certainly wonders if Paul's consigning the immoral member of the Corinthian church to Satan for the destruction of his sinful nature might fit this latter category (1 Corinthians 5:5).

Whatever the final resolution of some of these vexing issues, the Christian should not live in fear of the devil and demons. The simple exhortation of James still holds true: "Submit yourselves, then, to God. Resist the devil, and he will flee from you" (James 4:7). Whenever the servants of Christ find themselves on the cutting edge of spiritual warfare, they need not fear the battle. The Spirit of Christ will honor their faith and grant guidance and power for victory in His name.

Endnotes

[1]D. G. Reid, "Principalities and Powers," in *Dictionary of Paul and His Letters,* ed. Gerald F. Hawthorne, Ralph P. Martin, and Daniel G. Reid (Downers Grove, Ill.: InterVarsity Press, 1993), 747.

[2]See the helpful discussion in Horst Balz and Gerhard Schneider, eds., *Exegetical Dictionary of the New Testament,* vol. 1. English trans. (Grand Rapids: William B. Eerdmans Publishing Company, 1990), 297–298.

[3]C. Peter Wagner and F. Douglas Pennoyer, eds., *Wrestling with Dark Angels* (Ventura, Calif.: Regal Books, 1990), 73–91.

[4]C. Peter Wagner, *Blazing the Way* (Ventura, Calif.: Regal Books, 1995), 153–182.

[5]This reading of the Septuagint is preserved in a Qumran fragment (4QDt^q). See G. B. Caird, *New Testament Theology* (Oxford: Clarendon Press, 1994), 102; and F. F. Bruce, *The Epistle to the Hebrews,* New International Commentary on the New Testament, rev. ed. (Grand Rapids: William B. Eerdmans Publishing Co., 1990), 71.

[6]Ibid.

[7]Clinton E. Arnold, *Powers of Darkness* (Downers Grove, Ill.: InterVarsity Press, 1992), 125; see also his discussion on 187–189.

[8]Johannes P. Louw and Eugene A. Nida, eds., *Greek-English Lexicon of the New Testament: Based on Semantic Domains,* vol. 1, 2d ed. (New York: United Bible Societies, 1988–1989), 545.

[9]Leslie A. Shepard, *Encyclopedia of Occultism & Parapsychology,* 3d ed., (Detroit, London: Gale Research, Inc., 1991), 1:272.

[10]H. A. Virkler, "Demonic Influence and Psychopathology," *Baker's Encyclopedia of Psychology,* ed. David G. Benner (Grand Rapids: Baker Book House, 1985), 293–299.

[11]Merrill F. Unger, *Biblical Demonology* (Wheaton, Ill.: Scripture Press, 1952), 100.

[12]Merrill F. Unger, *Demons in the World Today* (Wheaton, Ill.: Tyndale House Publishers, 1971), 184.

[13]Frank and Ida Mae Hammond, *Pigs in the Parlor: A Practical Guide to Deliverance* (Kirkwood, Mo.: Impact Books, Inc., 1973), 136.

[14]Timothy M. Warner, *Spiritual Warfare: Victory Over the Powers of This Dark World* (Wheaton Ill.: Crossway Books, 1991), 80.

[15]Kenneth Hagin, *The Triumphant Church* (Tulsa, Okla.: Faith Library Publications, 1993), 95.

[16]See the study by Peter H. Davids, "A Biblical View of the Ralationship of Sin and the Fruits of Sin: Sickness, Demonization, Death, Natural Calamity," in *The Kingdom and the Power: Are Healing and the Spiritual Gifts Used by Jesus and the Early Church Meant for the Church Today?* ed. Gary S. Greig and Kevin N. Springer (Ventura,

Calif.: Regal Books, 1993), 130; Wayne Grudem, *Systematic Theology: An Introduction to Biblical Doctrine* (Grand Rapids: Zondervan Publishing House, 1994), 423; Merrill F. Unger, *What Demons Can Do to Saints* (Chicago: Moody Press, 1977), 86.

[17]Warner has perhaps the clearest statement of this view. See Timothy M. Warner, "An Evangelical Position on Bondage and Exorcism," in *Essays on Spiritual Bondage and Deliverance,* ed. Willard M. Swartley (Elkhart, Ind.: Institute of Mennonite Studies, 1988), 85.

[18]See the discussion in Millard J. Erickson, *Christian Theology* (Grand Rapids: Baker Book House, 1983–1985), 520–524.

[19]Compare such writers as Mark I. Bubeck, *The Adversary* (Chicago: Moody Press, 1975), 78–92; Richard F. Lovelace *Dynamics of Spiritual Life: An Evangelical Theology of Renewal* (Downers Grove, Ill.: InterVarsity Press, 1979), 137–144; and Warner, "Evangelical Positions," in *Essays,* 86.

[20]Paul G. Hiebert, "Spiritual Warfare: Biblical Perspectives," *Mission Focus* 20:3 (September 1992): 45.

[21]Thomas Finger and Willard Swartley, "Bondage and Deliverance . . . ," in *Essays on Spiritual Bondage*, 27.

9

Presence and Power in the Local Church

Gary A. Kellner

If your reading of Scripture convinces you that signs and wonders should happen today, you may wonder how they fit into the life of the church that you pastor. Most ministers know pastors and laypersons who have gone off the deep end. They have heard horror stories, like the pastor who taught his dog to speak in tongues, or the evangelist who prayed for the unborn children of pregnant women to be baptized in the Holy Spirit and then identified the kicks of the unborn as initial evidence. As a result of the weird and bizarre, many second- and third-generation Pentecostal ministers fear excesses that can embarrass and even debilitate the church. Consequently, the real question is how to incorporate signs and wonders into the life of contemporary American congregations without indulging the strange and spurious. This chapter seeks to encourage pastors and church leaders to develop a model of ministry that makes room for the supernatural in the local church and to suggest ways to nurture an environment in which the supernatural can occur.

Changing Perspectives

Changes in perspective, caused by paradigm shifts, have preceded every widespread renewal movement in history. The conviction of Martin Luther and the other Reformers that the Church desperately needed to rediscover the gospel and the meaning of salvation fueled the Protestant Reformation in the sixteenth century. Emphasis on individual conversion in the eighteenth century, articulated by Jonathan Edwards, the Wesleys, and George Whitefield, inspired the evangelical revivals that swept England, Germany, and Britain's North American colonies. Believers in the late nineteenth century sought a transforming experience, a baptism in the Holy Spirit, that would enable them to live a holy life, preach the gospel with greater power, and heal the sick, recapturing the vitality and impact of the Apostolic Church. The Pentecostal revival was the result.

Numerous indicators suggest a yearning for spiritual renewal.[1] But if American congregations are going to see greater manifestations of God's grace and power, church leaders must discover new paradigms for congregational life—approaches to how churches worship, evangelize, and minister to hurting people— that are biblically faithful and culturally relevant. Paradigms must be changed because (1) the mind-sets of many ministers and congregations do not provide an environment conducive to power ministry, and (2) the cultures that shape them are not stagnant—they are constantly moving and changing. What perspectives are necessary for a paradigm that encourages the supernatural?

The starting place is a core conviction about the meaning of the gospel. Too frequently, ministers and theologians in Western churches reduce salvation to God's forgiveness of sins as a result of the debt paid by Christ and appropriated through faith. Yet we need to think of the gospel in terms of both forgiveness of sins and deliverance from sin's power. Signs and wonders, then, as an essential part of the gospel, deliver people from the power of evil. This conception of the gospel must be the beginning, the middle, and the ending of our understanding of what God has done in Christ if we are to see manifestations of God's grace and power. The Church lacks "power ministry" because pastors and laypersons view healing and deliverance as something auxiliary to the gospel.

In fact, the gospel announces freedom to the captive and breaks all manner of oppression! As John Wimber explains, these signs and wonders were Jesus' "calling cards, proof that the kingdom of God had come."[2]

Once you reframe your understanding of the gospel, then you also must redefine the minister's role. Although most English translations render the Greek as "preacher" (see 1 Timothy 2:7; 2 Timothy 1:11), the minister is a "herald" of the Kingdom, God's rule on earth. In the Mediterranean world, a herald preceded a king, shouting or trumpeting good news. He proclaimed what was otherwise unknown. Paul said, "I was appointed a preacher [i.e., herald] and apostle." Thus for Paul the preacher is aptly termed a "herald."[3]

The heralds of the Kingdom are not entrusted with delicate missions; God commissions them to declare a message. They dare not alter the message. Heralds proclaim and shout their message in public places, as Jesus did in His hometown of Nazareth when He read from the scroll of the prophet Isaiah: "Good news to the poor . . . freedom for the prisoners and recovery of sight for the blind, . . . release [for] the oppressed, . . . the year of the Lord's favor" (Luke 4:18–19).

In this context, the herald declares the Year of Jubilee, the time of deliverance and restoration, which began with the appearance of Jesus Christ and continues to this day!

When empowered by the Spirit, we, like Jesus, bring deliverance through signs and wonders. However, most American pastors do not primarily see themselves as heralds. The minister as manager is the dominant model in the church in the United States and Canada. While many ministers see themselves as chief executive officers, they usually function as chief operations officers, who recruit, supervise, and problem solve. Managerial and business jargon permeates the vocabulary of American church leaders. Pastors find themselves absorbed in the details of institutional self-preservation and are more often managers than spiritual leaders. To a great degree, pastors function as the proprietors of small businesses, spending an inordinate amount of time managing personnel, programs, and budgets. As a result, the standards for measuring success have become overwhelmingly quantitative, which one writer calls "The three B's: bodies, bucks, and buildings."[4] Many pastors want to move into a more authentic New Testament ministry but feel trapped in the business role.

More recently, with the influence of the church growth movement, there has been an increased emphasis on leadership rather than management as the pastor's primary responsibility. Church growth experts provide an important corrective to models of ministry not conducive to the church's mission. The fact remains, however, that corporate managerial models undergird this approach to ministry more than New Testament ones and do not adequately emphasize aspects of the minister's work portrayed in biblical metaphors (e.g., shepherd, elder, father, messenger).[5] We will never see more of the miraculous until we rethink our role as ministers and how that affects the practice of ministry.

Clearly, the local church needs management. The New Testament acknowledges as much, but the American preoccupation with management is not faithful to the New Testament concept of ministry and, as a result, will not produce power ministry. Gospel ministry in the Early Church was fundamentally one of word and deed, as Paul declared, "My message and my preaching were not with wise and persuasive words, but with a demonstration of the Spirit's power, so that your faith might not rest on men's wisdom, but on God's power" (1 Corinthians 2:4). One of the reasons the Church is not more effective in confronting evil powers is because management is the predominant focus of so many pastors.

Pentecostals at the turn of the century understood Paul's declaration. They knew that people needed deliverance, and that they were proclaimers of a Jesus Christ who is the "same yesterday and today and forever" (Hebrews 13:8). Their public ministries focused on setting people free. We must do the same. This does not deny the value of any other type of ministry. It does, however, establish the context for everything that comes under the name of New Testament ministry.

If moving into power ministry requires renewed perspectives about the nature of the gospel and ministry, it also requires a change in our worldview.[6] Christians in Europe and North America tend to conceive reality according to a worldview inherited from the eighteenth-century Enlightenment. Nature is rational and can be understood through observation and analysis. People, then, are perceived as rational creatures or "computers with legs."[7] Our cultural inheritance in the West, therefore, predisposes us to discount and minimize the supernatural. Westerners rely heavily on scientific method for problem solving, approaching almost everything in natural terms, whether it be church management issues, counseling, or even the charismata of the Holy Spirit.[8]

Our brothers and sisters in the Early Church perceived reality in a very different way, much like those in the developing world today (i.e., Africa, Latin America, Asia) or anywhere prior to the eighteenth century. Believers in the premodern world and non-Western cultures live in a universe in which "the heavens hang low," where both God and evil powers are far more involved in this world than the modern Western worldview acknowledges.[9] In fact, the spiritual world is more real than the physical world, inasmuch as the physical world proceeds from the spiritual.[10] We must adjust our understanding of reality to take greater account of the supernatural. When assessing situations, you should not only look for the "reasonable explanation," but you should also consider the possibility that what you see is not all there is.

Reshaping Practice

Once your perspectives about the meaning of the gospel and the nature of ministry have changed, you must then reorder your priorities as a ministering person. This means thinking more intentionally about how you use your time and invest your energy. Is it really possible to move into power ministry if 80 percent of your working day as a pastor is spent in management tasks? If one desires a ministry of apostolic power, one must embrace apostolic priorities; as Peter stated, "'It would not be right for us to neglect the ministry of the word of God in order to wait on tables. . . . and [we] will give our attention to prayer and the ministry of the word'" (Acts 6:2–4). Clearly, the first priority for the minister is to be immersed in the Word and Spirit, which requires time.

Whether you are a senior pastor, evangelist, missionary, or staff member, you must determine in your mind who God is, what the gospel means, and what God has called you to do. The kingdom of God will never come through you until it is first born in you. If you are a senior pastor, the church will never become what the pastor is not. Hence, the cultivation of the Kingdom in the life of the pastor is his or her greatest priority. This is not to say that the pastor should cease giving attention to oversight, since that function is inherent in the pastoral role. The pastor, however, gains a new vantage point to guide his choices about the practice of ministry.

Changing your role as a pastor is more easily said than done, since such changes have implications for pastoral responsibilities and the use of time. American congregations have expectations of their pastors and traditions that cannot be ignored. Yet those expectations and traditions alone must not drive the life of the church. The mission of God must prioritize the life of the pastor and that of the congregation. Every effective leader knows that changing the culture of an organization takes considerable time, tact, and effort. This is no less true in the church. The pastor who wants to see signs and wonders evaluates the services and ministries of the church by a model that measures effectiveness not by attendance but by whether people experience the transforming power of the gospel.

After taking the first step of reordering priorities, one must nurture the congregational environment. The ecology of the local congregation must be congenial to the supernatural, an environment that inspires faith and provides space for the Holy Spirit to operate. Signs and wonders do not always occur in such an environment, but they seldom occur anywhere else. Nurturing such an environment involves several things.

First, pastors must cultivate the presence of God in the public services of the congregation. Pastor Tommy Reid of the Full Gospel Tabernacle, Buffalo, New York, speaks eloquently to this point: "I used to believe that the role of the pastor was to be a bringer of truth. I have come to realize that that was not right, but that the role of the pastor is to be a conveyor of Presence, and in the atmosphere of Presence, proclaim the truth."[11] When we talk about "Presence" we are not talking about omnipresence, that divine attribute by which God is in, over, and under all that is. In Scripture, the presence of God is a special manifestation whereby God's people become particularly aware that He is with them for a purpose. The burning bush and the cloud by day and the pillar of fire by night that accompanied the Children of Israel from Egypt to the Promised Land illustrate this.

Perhaps the most critical element in nurturing an environment of the supernatural lies in cultivating Presence, because people perceive truth in the atmosphere of Presence. Israel learned this at Sinai and at the dedication of Solomon's Temple.

The manifestation of God's presence—His greatness and glory—overwhelmed the people, transcending ritual or words. Through these divine moments, the Israelites came to know God in a more profound way because they had experienced Him.

Likewise, the events that transpired on the Day of Pentecost illustrate this point. What happened? As the people of God heard the sound like a rushing, mighty wind, they became aware that God was coming into that place with power, that something signal was about to happen. When they saw the cloven tongues of fire sit upon each person, they recognized that God had distributed His power to each one. And as they began to speak distinct languages otherwise unknown to them, they realized that their own praise to God, and subsequently their witness, became bolder and more persuasive.

In the atmosphere of Presence, believers, including ministers, realize that God is among them and that when God is present, anything can happen. Our Lord said as much: "For where two or three come together in my name, there am I with them" (Matthew 18:20). Even the most casual reading of the New Testament suggests that wherever Jesus appeared, all that God does became possible. The supernatural occurs in this kind of atmosphere.

In order to cultivate Presence, we need to restructure worship services. If elements in the worship service distract or diminish our sense of Presence, we need to reconsider their place in the service. How many times have you attended a service in which the atmosphere was thick with the presence of God, only to have the announcements, the offering, or a baby dedication squelch the moment? The moment of power slips away. Rarely in a single service do you ever regain that special quality. We must come to see the manifestation of God's presence as a window of opportunity for the supernatural. It is a moment in time when a congregation is focused, when they are in one accord. You must seize the moment because it seldom lasts long. You must be prepared to set aside the order of service and give the Holy Spirit room to operate. That may mean permitting silence or ministering healing or inviting people to experience the transformation of conversion.

On the first night of the "Signs and Wonders" conference, worship leader "Big John" Hall said to a congregation of three thousand ministers and laypersons, "We have an agenda; it's a definite maybe."[12] That openness to divine contingency established the tone for the entire conference. I am not suggesting that we eliminate a planned agenda for corporate worship; I am saying that it needs to be an interruptible agenda.

Second, not only should pastors cultivate the presence of God, but they must also nurture the congregational environment through preaching. Reflecting on the transformation of first-century pagans from darkness into light, Paul attributed it to the gospel of Christ, "because it is the power of God for the salvation of everyone who believes" (Romans 1:16). As people in darkness hear the gospel, they begin to see "a great light" (Matthew 4:16), the possibility of a life of grace and freedom. Preaching is identified second not because it is less important but because in the atmosphere of Presence, preaching becomes effective. If unbelief permeates the atmosphere, the potential for the supernatural is limited, as Jesus himself experienced at Nazareth (Matthew 13:58).

When the atmosphere has not been prepared by the manifestation of Presence, preaching often becomes an exercise in futility and frustration. Acts 2 suggests a pattern for understanding the relationship of Presence to preaching. In an atmosphere prepared by the powerful manifestation of God's presence, Peter, inspired and emboldened by the experience of Presence, preached his Pentecost sermon, in which the people "were cut to the heart and said to Peter and the other apostles, 'Brothers, what shall we do?'" (Acts 2:37). The proclamation of the Word in an atmosphere of Presence is essential if we would see signs and wonders, because through preaching, people become aware of what God has done in and through His Son, and they experience what He can do.

People in the church need to hear this proclamation as much as those outside because "faith comes from hearing the message, and the message is heard through the word of Christ" (Romans 10:17). They may need healing or deliverance from satanic attack. Further, there are also people in every church who are captive to patterns of thinking shaped by their environment and by destructive life experiences. These patterns of bondage can be broken only through the preaching of the Word of God. The preaching that releases the captives has little to do with what so often goes by that name in the contemporary church. It is neither the gospel of self-help, nor the auto-soteriology of psychobabble. It is not what some preachers mistakenly call expository preaching: a dry, dusty running commentary of Scripture, which treats the Word of God like an object to be studied rather than a dynamic reality to be experienced. Jesus said, " 'The words I have spoken to you are spirit and they are life' " (John 6:63).

Preaching that emphasizes transformation and deliverance nurtures an environment for signs and wonders. It may have elements of teaching in it; however, it is not primarily instructional. It will certainly deal with life's problems, but it is not problem centered. In the last decade, it has been popular to preach to life's hurts. That kind of emphasis makes problems great and God small. Proclamational preaching in an atmosphere of Presence gives people the sense of God's greatness and that with Him all things are possible.

Third, a different use of time nurtures an environment for signs and wonders. When God manifests himself, it is important to stop and consider what He is doing. This is not to say that services should go on endlessly, yet the supernatural occurs most frequently in an atmosphere where we provide space for God to manifest His grace and His power. This simply takes time. Historically, Pentecostals did this primarily in what they called "the altar service," a time following the ministry of the Word that often ran as long or longer than the sermon. It was an occasion for response. Providing space should not be restricted to the altar service, but whenever a divine incursion takes place.

Finally, nurturing an environment conducive to the supernatural requires encouraging the charismata. In 1 Corinthians 12:7, the apostle Paul described the charismata as the "manifestation of the Spirit," literally the shining forth of the Spirit. In part, the function of what Pentecostals and charismatics call the "gifts of the Spirit" is to indicate that the Spirit of God is present and to make known the specific work He wants to do. Through the charismata, the Spirit's agenda for a particular moment in time becomes known.

The late Donald Gee, an eminent British Pentecostal leader, once expressed the desire that Pentecostals be truly worthy of the name and that all the operations of the Spirit would be frequent in their services—not just tongues, interpretation of tongues, and prophecy.[13] When considering power ministry, one has to move beyond the vocal gifts, since they represent only one dimension of the Spirit's activity in the congregation. For dealing with congenital disorders, chronic disease, or terminal illness, the charismata of healing is needed, as well as a surge of faith. At times what appears to be a psychological problem or an illness is actually demonic activity, in which case, discerning of spirits is needed.

In practical terms, how can the pastor encourage charismata? First, the pastor must bring people into an awareness of the significance of the baptism in the Holy Spirit as an experience that *immerses* people in the Spirit and empowers them for ministry, even as it did the first Christians.[14] When persons are immersed in or saturated with the Spirit of God, they become more acutely aware of the Spirit's operations. And if they have been properly instructed as to the purpose of the baptism in the Holy Spirit, they will be more confident when the Spirit does begin to operate in and through them.

Second, the pastor must also let the congregation know the importance of the charismata in the life of the congregation. This can be done through teaching; however, it is important not to limit our concept of teaching to a single sermon or a series on the subject (although this is a good starting point). The most important teaching is done through modeling in services, by demonstrating openness and hunger, but also by verbally encouraging people to respond to the promptings of the Holy Spirit. Here, the pastor must function as a coach, exhorting members of the body and affirming them, even when they make mistakes—especially when they make mistakes. This calls for a great deal of tenderness and patience.

Recently, I was in a conference and an individual began to wail and dominate the service during a corporate time of intercession. In what may have been one of the most sensitive responses I have ever heard, one of the leaders stopped him and said, "Brother, I sense that God is moving inside of you in a very deep and profound way, and I affirm that. But I also sense that's not what God is doing in the service right now, so I want to ask you to hold that intercession and let me share what I think the Lord is saying."

Developing a Congregational Model

Everyone operates with some model of ministry, whether or not it is explicitly stated or even recognized. As you move into power ministry, you must develop a model that is faithful to the Christ revealed in Scripture, consistent with your own calling, and culturally relevant. A variety of approaches have proven effective. Traditional Pentecostals have tended to operate in a pastor-centered model in the local church, while neo-Pentecostals have focused more on the role of the laity. More recently, John Wimber has emphasized the training of ministry teams within the congregation.[15] It is hard to make the case that one of these models should be embraced to the exclusion of the others.

In developing a congregational model, the pastor needs to focus on an important New Testament value: an authentic model of ministry encourages the full participation of the body of Christ. It is inclusive, not exclusive. The healing movement of the 1940s and 1950s demonstrated the danger of focusing power ministry on individuals. Many Christians came to the conclusion that the only way to experience healing was to be prayed for by a certain evangelist. Rather than allowing Christ's power to heal, the fixation with personalities inhibited the release of healing power in many congregations.

C. Peter Wagner offers a useful model for helping individuals identify and develop their spiritual gifts. This model can be adapted as you develop a congregational model for power ministry.[16] The first step explores the possibilities. Pastors should help Christians acquaint themselves with the various ways the Spirit operates. The second step is to experiment. Believers need to be encouraged to respond when they sense that the Spirit might be manifesting one of the charismata. Some Pentecostals are very uncomfortable with the idea of experimenting with spiritual things. They operate with the notion that only when God speaks directly to them can they do anything. This can be paralyzing. They need flexibility and a willingness to risk. Third, Wagner suggests believers examine their feelings. He does not argue that a person should rely exclusively on feelings, but a sense of joy and enthusiasm in ministering a particular spiritual gift may often indicate the Spirit's activity in that person's life. Fourth, he recommends that the person evaluate his or her effectiveness. Are particular manifestations making a difference in the lives of individuals and the congregation? Fifth, Wagner urges believers to expect confirmation from the Body. If a ministry is valid, it should be recognized and affirmed by the body of Christ. Most pastors of Pentecostal and charismatic congregations have suffered with lone rangers, highly individualistic persons who function as independent power centers in the congregation.

Paul's guidelines in 1 Corinthians 14 for manifesting the charismata clearly indicate that evaluating spiritual gifts is essential to the health of the congregation.[17] Whether you follow Wagner's model or not, you need to evaluate the effectiveness of any approach to power ministry.

Before anyone implements a model of ministry, it is important to remember that power ministry is not a form of technology. It is easy to fall into the trap that our words and methods carry efficacy. They do not! It is Christ who heals; it is Christ who delivers! A model helps us structure our approach to ministry. But like Ezekiel's valley of dry bones, any approach is lifeless unless invigorated by the Spirit.

Overcoming Problems

Due to the high octane nature of signs and wonders and human fallenness, there will be problems. Things will get messy because many people, including those who are dysfunctional, may be drawn to the supernatural. The rush of excitement that accompanies manifestations of divine power will cause uninstructed people and selfish people to act foolishly. As long as spiritual births are taking place, there will be immature children in the family, and there will be those who become preoccupied with gifts and manifestations. There will be excesses. There will be failures. There will be a loss of control at times.

Some leaders deal with potential problems by backing away from signs and wonders. They fear the excesses and the loss of control, concluding it is better to play it safe. Consequently, they never see the fullness of what God can do. Until your confidence in God is greater than your fear of problems, you will never press into the kind of ministry that breaks Satan's stronghold in a city and brings release to the captives, recovery of sight to the blind, and liberty to the oppressed.

This is not to say that you simply let people run amuck. God gives the responsibility to pastors to provide oversight of the congregation through the ministries of preaching and teaching—to instruct, exhort, reprove, and correct. The pastor also provides leadership in the worship service by leading and guiding the congregation as the Spirit moves. The pastor's role is to provide center-stream ministry for the church, to work to bring balance and health to the body of Christ. Here, too, great care and sensitivity must be exercised. The move of God in the congregation is a very fragile thing. If a pastor speaks too quickly or harshly, he or she runs the risk of wounding people, and when that happens, the congregation grows reactive and becomes less open to the working of the Spirit.

An old African proverb instructs one in how to hold an egg. If you hold it too tightly, you will crush it. If you hold it too loosely, it will fall to the ground. The only way to hold an egg is lightly.[18] The same is true when it comes to handling the problems that inevitably accompany signs and wonders.

Endnotes

[1]Indicators in the 1990s include citywide prayer meetings like the Pastors' Prayer Summits in Portland, Oregon, and David Bryant's "Concerts of Prayer." In the winter and spring of 1995, prayer revivals occurred on college and seminary campuses (e.g., Howard Payne University, Wheaton College, and Southwestern Baptist Theological Seminary). The "Signs and Wonders" conference sponsored by the Assemblies of God Theological Seminary in March 1995 attracted more than one thousand senior pastors, many of whom have reported a transformation in their own lives and, subsequently, in the congregations they serve.

[2]John Wimber, *Power Evangelism* (San Francisco: Harper & Row, Publishers, 1986), 91.

[3]Colin Brown, ed., *The New International Dictionary of New Testament Theology* (Grand Rapids: Zondervan Publishing House, 1978), 3:48–57.

[4]Bill Hull, *The Disciple Making Pastor* (Old Tappan, N.J.: Fleming H. Revell, 1988), 12.

[5]Brown, *New International Dictionary,* 3:564–369; Geoffrey W. Bromiley, ed., *The International Standard Bible Encyclopedia* (Grand

Rapids: William B. Eerdmans Publishing Company, 1982), 2:53–54; Brown, *New International Dictionary,* 3:614–621; David Noel Freeman, ed., *The Anchor Bible Dictionary* (New York: Doubleday, 1992), 6:644–653.

[6]Clifford Geertz describes a people's worldview as "their picture of the way things in sheer actuality are, their concept of nature, of self, of society. It contains their most comprehensive ideas of order." Clifford Geertz, *Interpretation of Cultures* (New York: Basic Books, Inc., 1973), 127.

[7]Martin Marty, "Entertaining Angels: Spirituality in the 90's," lecture at Southwest Missouri State University, Springfield, Mo., November 2, 1995.

[8]By developing "gift profiles," administering exams like the Modified Houts, and also by analyzing the linguistic content of glossalalia, many charismatics, Pentecostals, and Third Wavers certainly show the influence of Western thought forms.

[9]David Hall, *Worlds of Wonder, Days of Judgment: Popular Religious Belief in Early New England* (New York: Alfred A. Knopf, 1989), 71–80.

[10]To assert the priority of the supernatural is not to deny that scientific method has its values—as the scientific and technological advances of the last two centuries attest—or to suggest that we should return to a primitivist worldview. Rationality is needed to organize a society, a school, or to perform a medical procedure. Nevertheless, many things cannot be explained by scientific method—humor and pathos, hope and despair, faith and fear.

[11]Tommy Reid, interview by author, Springfield, Mo., March 9, 1995.

[12]John Hall, "Signs and Wonders" conference, cassette #95SWC37/761107 (Springfield, Mo.: March 6, 1995).

[13]Donald Gee, *Concerning Spiritual Gifts* (Springfield, Mo.: Gospel Publishing House, 1949), 27.

[14]To emphasize the importance of a distinct experience of Spirit baptism is not to say that the Holy Spirit cannot manifest himself through any believer as He chooses, but that this experience enhances the sensitivity of the believer to the work of the Holy Spirit.

[15]See John Wimber, *Power Healing* (San Francisco: Harper & Row, Publishers, 1987).

[16]C. Peter Wagner, *Your Spiritual Gifts Can Help Your Church Grow* (Ventura, Calif.: Regal Books, 1982).

[17]C. Peter Wagner, *Your Church Can Grow: Seven Vital Signs of a Healthy Church* (Ventura, Calif.: Regal Books, 1976), 73–74.

[18]Del Tarr, *Double Image: Biblical Insights from African Parables* (Mahwah, N.J.: Paulist Press, 1994), 32.